DATE DUE

SEP 2 9 1995	
NOV 1 4 1995	
APR _ 1 1996	
APRIL 14	
FEB 1 0 1997	
APR _ 3 1997	
~~S OCT 22 1110~~	
~~Oct 21 97~~	
NOV 2 2 1997	
MAY _ 7 2001	
OCT 2 8 2001	
FEB 0 2 2004	

BRODART   Cat. No. 23-221

The Joy of Suffering

Psychoanalytic Theory and Therapy of Masochism

Shirley Panken, Ph.D.

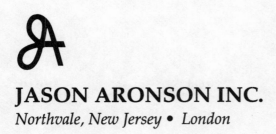

JASON ARONSON INC.

Northvale, New Jersey • London

THE MASTER WORK SERIES

Copyright © 1993, 1983, 1973 by Jason Aronson

First softcover edition 1993

Library of Congress Cataloging-in-Publication Data

Panken, Shirley.
    The joy of suffering.

        Bibliography: p. 223
        Include index.
        1. Psychic masochism.   I. Title.
    RC553.M36P36   1984   616.85′835   83-15841
    ISBN 1-56821-120-1

Manufactured in the United States of America. Jason Aronson Inc. offers books and cassettes. For information and catalog write to Jason Aronson Inc., 230 Livingston Street, Northvale, New Jersey 07647.

Contents

PREFACE TO THE NEW PRINTING V

PREFACE 1

ACKNOWLEDGMENTS 9

  I. INTRODUCTION 11

 II. FREUD'S EVOLVING THEORIES ON MASOCHISM 17

III. FURTHER CONTRIBUTIONS TO THE LITERATURE ON
     MASOCHISM 31

IV. CLINICAL ILLUSTRATIONS 63

 V. DEVELOPMENTAL PATTERNS IN MASOCHISTIC
     BEHAVIOR 81

VI.   DIFFERENTIAL DIAGNOSIS 95

VII.   THE ROLE OF SADISM OR AGGRESSION IN
      MASOCHISM 107

VIII.   THE PLEASURE IN PAIN 127

IX.   PSYCHOTHERAPY AND MASOCHISM 143

X.   CULTURAL IMPLICATIONS OF MASOCHISTIC
     PHENOMENA 197

REFERENCES 223

INDEX 235

Preface to the New Printing

In my study of masochism, I seek answers to a series of controversial questions. The first is "What are the unique characteristics in the individual's life history, particularly in the parent–child and family constellation, that make imperative the recourse to masochistic behavior?"

An analysis of masochistic formations in my patients focuses on their sense of oral and tactile deprivation, deeply embedded in the mother–infant relationship, stemming from the mother's ambivalent, alternately withholding and engulfing attitudes. The mother's emotional availability remains inconsistent so that early masochistic predilections continue to reverberate in the succeeding critical developmental phases, creating dissonances in optimal growth of ego functions. Masochistic self-devaluation, feelings of humiliation, damage and narcissistic injury, imprinted by incorporation of the "unconscious, negative expectations" of the mother, serve as defensive structure, with the intent to accommodate and preserve the relationship with mother by ego constriction and failure. There is no conscious awareness of the deprivation and meagerness of the maternal relationship.

In updating the literature on masochism since 1983, one notes greater emphasis on the effects of psychological and physical trauma in infancy and their reverberations in the later development of masochistic behavior. Glenn (1984a) states that painful experiences, such as object loss or separation, that occur before object constancy in preoedipal infancy can be the basis for the development of masochism. Glenn also refers to instances of psychic trauma in children (1984b), described as a "flooding of stimulation from within and without" so overwhelming that the child cannot utilize his/her usual defenses and becomes prone to a masochistic orientation. The masochism or self-inflicted suffering is exacerbated when the trauma (serious injury, illness or surgery, psychic loss, or emotional abuse) plus the infant's or child's feelings of pain, neediness, helplessness, or aggression, are insensitively nuanced or inappropriately responded to by the parent (Grossman 1991, Herzog 1983). As an adult, the individual may attempt mastery by repeating the traumatic event in a controlled and modified form.

Galenson (1988) finds that psychopathology in the infant is concomitant to the mother's conflicts concerning aggression. The mother's nonacceptance of the infant's "normal hostile aggression" (McDevitt 1983) may result in a preponderance of teasing and subsequent introduction of sadomasochism in the mother–child interplay, beginning in the early months and particularly visible by the second year. In this framework, the child identifies with the mother as aggressor. When the child's rage is heightened however, the relationship with the mother is at risk. The child's hostile aggression may become self-directed, manifested in self-biting and hair-pulling. According to Novick and Novick (1987), hair pulling represents the infant's or child's attempt to substitute for the mother's withdrawal, that is, the need for the object supersedes the need for pleasure.

As the child capitulates to the mother's aggression, continues Galenson (1988), the child at first appears to "avoid" the mother but eventually becomes increasingly passive, inhibited, and regressed, reflected in various manifestations of "protomasochism" at the early genital phase. Loewenstein (1957) first described "protomasochism" as the mechanism of "seduction of the aggressor," the infant's or child's "normal" predilection for situations involving danger or fear, obviously encouraged by the "erotic complicity" of the parent.

Novick and Novick (1987), in examining the development of "fixed" beating fantasies in children and adults, found mother-infant disturbances in the earliest months. Postoedipally, masochistic or pain-seeking behavior appears as conscious or unconscious fantasy serving multiple ego functions, and takes the form, though not necessarily the content, of the beating fantasy. In the fantasy, the patient is an innocent victim who, through pain or suffering, achieves "reunion with the object, defense against aggressive destruction and loss of the object, avoidance of narcissistic pain, and instinctual gratification by fantasy participation in the oedipal situation." This fantasy is, in the authors' view, the "essence of masochism."

Seelig and Person (1991), in their reconstruction of a patient's early life, focus on the development of a "rageful sadomasochistic transference," evidencing problems in the rapprochement phase of separation-individuation. They connect the patient's tumultous transference to a rejection of both pre-oedipal and oedipal "triangulation" perpetuating a "hostile-dependent" mother–child relationship and resulting in the patient's unconscious belief that sadomasochistic interactions are the chief means of achieving a close relationship. The authors convey that the patient via her sadomasochistic defenses achieves narcissistic repair, erotization of suffering, and regulation of self-esteem. In their view, surrender and masochism, domination and sadism, are "perverse characterological adaptations" that retain "mutuality." In short, "sadomasochistic pathology" permits "intimate though distorted human contact."

Here, skepticism and a questioning of values are in order concerning the use of the terms *intimate* and *mutuality* in regard to sadomasochistic interactions possibly involving authoritarian or destructive behavior.

Other questions I ask are, "How do masochistic individuals cope with aggression? Is the masochist both sadist and sufferer, that is, sadomasochistic? Or is this a misleading merger of two distinct entities?" A related question I ask is: "What is meant by the merging of pain and pleasure, that is, the 'joy' of suffering?"

My contention has been that the masochist and the sadist differ in both character structure and intrapsychic dynamics. In each, aggression has vastly different meanings regarding self and other. In my study, masochistic patients are rarely conscious of anger or rebelliousness concerning parental figures. Their hostility is masked or channeled into psychosomatic symptoms. Recourse to self-aggrandizing or self-debasing fantasies or dreams is seen, but dependency and reparative needs plus fear of separation are the crucial motivational forces. One may posit a spectrum of masochistic attitudes ranging from the muted, acquiescent, enslaved individual seeking punishment to the demanding, provocative, complaining person who projects hostility onto others. Yet the underlying feelings of powerlessness and weakness are similar. Brenman (1952) emphasizes the central role of projective mechanisms in some varieties of masochistic behavior, the need to defend oneself against hostile impulses.

In my view, the sadistic personality, recipient of more extreme forms of early abandonment and often brutal exploitation by parents, also possesses an underlying weak, impotent, and crippled sense of self. In contrast to the masochist, however, the sadist lives aggressively and destructively through others, needs to subjugate and humiliate his/her partner, and is preoccupied with control, violence, and power.

I further question the concept of seeking "pleasure" in pain or humiliation. Conceivably, what might be meant is a need for heightened tension and sensation, a need to feel vitalized and validated. Masochistic personalities "enjoy" suffering as little as others do. In the masochist, satisfactions are restricted, self-assertion avoided and, when attempted, are concomitant to considerable anxiety, obliterating all pleasurable feelings.

Masochistic phenomena deal not so much with "pleasure" in pain as repetition of early situations involving abuse, defeat, neglect, the gamut of negative attention, the seeking of "ill-treatment as though it were love" (Berliner 1958). However, constitutional or temperamental predisposition, threshhold of frustration tolerance, intensity of need and activity level, and trauma of hospitalization and surgery in childhood also play a role in early imprinting or pain constellations. When there is duality of pleasure and pain, it may be best understood in biological and constitutional terms according to Grossman (1986), and according to Caston's (1984) reporting of a panel on masochism, citing the contributions of Asch and those of Gedo.

Updating the literature, the terms *sadism* and *masochism* are used interchangeably. Emphasis has remained as in the past, on the belief that sadism and masochism inhere in one person and that there is pleasure in the infliction of pain. The following articles were part of a panel discussion in 1988 that explored variegated aspects of sadomasochism:

Kernberg (1991) has long promulgated the belief, following Freud and Klein, that sadomasochism is inherent in infantile sexuality and is related to what he believes is "erotized" body contact in relation to the early mother–child ministrations. Kernberg further believes that sadomasochism as part of one's conscious or unconscious fantasies plays an essential role in "normal" sexual behavior and love relationships in both sexes and is central to sexual excitement. It is his belief that sexual excitement is a "basic affect preventing the primitive splitting of love and hate"; unconscious components of sexual excitement are found in "aggressive penetration and intermingling, the desire to both transgress oedipal prohibitions and the secretiveness of the primal scene, the wish to penetrate the boundaries of a teasing and withholding partner." Sadomasochism, he states, represents the aggressive behavior elicited in the framework of frustration by an idealized mother. Kernberg's orientation seems similar to Stoller's (1985) conception of sadomasochism as an "erotic form of hatred."

It is my belief (Panken 1979) that the masochistic rather than sadistic paradigm is more typical of the prolonged dependency of childhood despite the sadistic inevitabilities attributed to the child's oral, anal, phallic, and genital psychosexual development. To my mind, the mother's early caretaking, patterns of touching, stroking, holding, rocking, and emotional communication in general are not necessarily "erotized"; nor is expectable frustration by the mother reacted to with anger and rage in "good enough mothering." In addition, "normal" sexual relations are not permeated with conscious or unconscious sadomasochistic fantasy or sadomasochistic behavior.

Rothstein (1991) places sadomasochism in the category of compromise formations, which include enactments, perversions, characterological manifestations, self-torturing, and obsessive fantasies — emanating from "drive derivatives, affects, defenses, and self-punitive behavior." Rothstein stresses the impact of the object world in shaping individual character and therefore in the genesis of masochistic, narcissistic, and sadistic fantasies.

Chasseguet-Smirgel (1991) belives sadomasochism reflects the anal modality wherein the individual "aims to destroy reality," equated with the paternal universe, and aims to obliterate any recognition of sexual and generational differences, namely, the fact that the mother and father possess procreative sexuality and the child does not.

Blos (1991) perceives neurotic sadomasochism as a fantasied means to retain bisexuality and avoid the disappointment in feeling limited to one gender.

In an overview article, Blum (1991) alludes to the still "elusive and mysterious" meaning of sadomasochism:

Sadism and masochism are today considered to be complex compromise formations, overdetermined, with multiple functions probably arising from all phases of development. Sadomasochistic phenomena, ubiquitous and universal, represent gratification, defense, and adaptation and an important dimension of self and object relations. All psychic structures contribute to sadomasochistic compromise formations. [p. 432]

His formulation here is similar to an earlier integration by Brenman (1952) in terms of the concept of "motivational hierarchy," a many-leveled starting point for analyzing any complex psychological phenomenon. Blum acknowledges that there is a continuing controversy as to whether sadomasochism is a unitary concept, then asserts he is unable to encompass one without the other. He believes the masochistic individual always fantasizes a sadistic partner. Reverting again, he agrees there is a difference between patients manifesting self-defeating, self-induced suffering, and those who torture or inflict suffering onto others and in so doing may be "dangerous or violent to family and society." In elucidating the "goal" of sadomasochism, Blum, following Brenner (1959), suggests that without sexual pleasure in suffering, masochism would not differ from passive aggression, self-abasement, and self-defeat. Blum seems wavering in his insistence on the fusion of masochism and sadism.

A further question in my study of masochism deals with the relationship between masochism and other diagnostic entities. Regarding the literature on the difficulties inherent in diagnosing a patient as masochistic character or depression, Caston (1984) indicates that it is of importance to clarify the difference between the clinical picture of each. The need to suffer is of no value as a diagnostic consideration unless one knows "toward what end and gratification."

Stolorow and Lachmann (1981) explore the connection of masochistic and sadistic formations to the narcissistic dimension. This involves "restoring and sustaining the cohesion, stability and positive affective coloring of a precarious, threatened, damaged or fragmenting self-representation." Here is is the quality of preoedipal developmental damage and narcissistic injury that affects the degree to which the individual resorts to "primitive sexualization" or "aggressivization."

Cooper (1988) believes narcissism and masochism are closely linked and he launches the term *narcissistic-masochistic character*. In "normal" development the infant endows whatever is familiar with pleasure, whether these are "painful experiences or depriving mothers". In Cooper's view, painful body experiences, especially skin impingements, help define body-image and self-image, as well as further the process of self-definition and separation-individuation. When early narcissistic injuries are cumulative and intense, "disappointment and refusal" become preferred means of narcissistic assertion; narcissistic and masochistic distortions permeate the personality structure, exerting fantasied control over a cruel and degrading mother. Here the pleasure sought is preoedipal, not genital-sexual. With prevailing narcissistic-masochistic pathology, superego distortion and harshness also dominate the clinical picture.

Since Cooper's concept of narcissism refers to both self-inflation and self-diminution, his use of designation, "narcissistic-masochistic character" is ambiguous.

Numerous articles seek to fathom various diagnostic and psychodynamic issues concerning masochism and sadism, namely those by Akhtar (1991), Grossman (1986), Levin (1990), Maleson (1984), Sacks (1991), and Simons (1987). Multiple perspectives on masochism are noted in Glick and Meyers' (1988) book, with essays offering variegated approaches to the treatment and understanding of masochism in the framework of current developments in psychoanalytic research and theory. Baumeister's (1989) book perceives masochism as a "powerful escape from self," an eradication of the individual's awareness of his/her normal identity. The point of view of the essays in the book edited by Montgomery and Greif (1989) suggests that the masochistic patient is embedded in a "world of pain and surrender," the goal to "stay alive and attached" avoiding the tilt toward "identity diffusion, psychotic regression and suicide."

It is of decisive importance that the child cling to the parent to maintain some form of contact, the parent's negative and rejecting responses notwithstanding, since the danger of withdrawal or abandonment is catastrophic. Masochistic behavior is a means of placating the parent, though frequently, the child's unconsciously propelled provacativeness perpetuates the masochistic interplay, eliciting further punitiveness from the very person from whom affection is sought, thus reinforcing the sadomasochistic cycle. To my mind, the manner in which sadism and masochism are intertwined has to do not so much with fusion of drives as with complexly orchestrated interactions and relationships wherein the underlying characterological patterns and motivational structures differ for the masochist and for the sadist.

REFERENCES

Akhtar, S. (1991). Sadomasochism in the perversions. *J. Am. Psychoanal. Assoc.* 39:741-756.

Baumeister, R. F. (1989). *Masochism and the Self.* Hillsdale, NJ: Lawrence Erlbaum.

Berliner, B. (1958). The role of object relations in moral masochism. *Psychoanal. Q.* 27:38-56.

Blos, Jr., P. (1991). Sadomasochism and the defense against recall of painful affect. *J. Am. Psychoanal. Assoc.* 39:417-430.

Blum, H., (1991). Sadomasochism in the psychoanalytic process, within and beyond the pleasure principle. *J. Am. Psychoanal. Assoc.* 39:431-450.

Brenman, M. (1952). On teasing and being teased and the problems of moral masochism. *The Psychoanalytic Study of the Child.* 7:264-265. New York: International Universities Press.

Brenner, C. (1959). The masochistic character. *J. Am. Psychoanal. Assoc.* 7:197-226.

Caston, J. (1984). The relationship between masochism and depression. *J. Am. Psychoanal. Assoc.* 32:603-614.

Chasseguet-Smirgel, J. (1991). Sadomasochism in the perversions: some thoughts on the destruction of reality. *J. Am. Psychoanal. Assoc.* 39:399-416.

Cooper, A. (1988). The narcissistic character. In *Masochism: Current Psychoanalytic Perspectives*, ed. R. A. Glick and D. I. Meyers, pp. 93-116. Hillsdale, NJ: The Analytic Press.

Galenson, E. (1988). The precursors of masochism: protomasochism. In *Masochism: Current Psychoanalytic Perspectives*, ed. R. A. Glick and D. I. Meyers, pp. 189-204. Hillsdale, NJ: The Analytic Press.

Glenn, J. (1984a). A note on loss, pain and masochism in children. *J. Am. Psychoanal. Assoc.* 32:63-74.

———— (1984b). Psychic trauma and masochism. *J. Am. Psychoanal. Assoc.* 32:357-386.

Glick, R. A., and Meyers, D. I., eds. (1988). In Introduction, *Masochism: Current Psychoanalytic Perspectives*, pp. 1-26. Hillsdale, NJ: The Analytic Press.

Grossman, W. (1986). Notes on masochism: a discussion of the history and development of a psychoanalytic concept. *Psychoanal. Q.* 45:379-413.

_____ (1991). Pain, aggression, fantasy and concepts of sadomasochism. *Psychoanal. Q.* 50:22–52.

Herzog, J. M. (1983). A neonatal intensive care syndrome: a pain complex involving neuroplasticity and psychic trauma. In *Frontiers of Infant Psychiatry*, ed. J. D. Call et al., pp. 291–300. New York: Basic Books.

Kernberg, O. (1991). Sadomasochism, sexual excitement, and perversion. *J. Am. Psychoanal. Assoc.* 39:333–362.

Levin, F. M. (1990). Sadism and masochism in neurosis and symptom formation. *J. Am. Psychoanal. Assoc.* 38:789–804.

Loewenstein, R. M. (1957). A contribution to the psychoanalytic theory of masochism. *J. Am. Psychoanal. Assoc.* 5:197–234.

Maleson, F. G. (1984). The multiple meanings of masochism in psychic discourse. *J. Am. Psychoanal. Assoc.* 32:325–356.

McDevitt, J. B. (1983). The emergence of hostile aggression and its defensive and adaptive modifications during the separation-individuation process. *J. Am. Psychoanal. Assoc.* 31:273–300.

Montgomery, J. D., and Greif, A. C., eds. (1989). *Masochism: The Treatment of Self-Inflicted Suffering*. Madison, CT: International Universities Press.

Novick, K. K., and Novick, J. (1987). The essence of masochism. *Psychoan. Study of the Child* 42:353–384. New York: International Universities Press.

Panken, S. (1979). Issues in sadomasochism devolving on ego psychology and object relations theory. In *Integrating Ego Psychology and Object Relations*, ed. L. Saretsky, G. D. Goldman, and D. S. Millman, pp. 81–96. Dubuque, IA: Kendall/Hunt.

Rothstein, A. (1991). Sadomasochism in the neuroses conceived of as a pathological compromise formation. *J. Am. Psychoanal. Assoc.* 39:363–376.

Sacks, M. H. (1991). Sadism and masochism in character disorder and resistance. *J. Am. Psychoanal. Assoc.* 39: 215–226.

Seelig, B. J., and Person, E. S. (1991). A sadomasochistic transference: its relation to distortions in the rapprochement subphase. *J. Am. Psychoanal. Assoc.* 39:939–966.

Simons, R. J. (1987). Contributions to psychiatric nosology: forms of masochistic behavior. *J. Am. Psychoanal. Assoc.* 35:583–608.

Stoller, R. (1985). *Observing the Erotic Imagination*. New Haven, CT: Yale University Press.

Stolorow, R. D., and Lachmann, F. M. (1981). *Psychoanalysis of Developmental Arrests: Theory and Treatment*. New York: International Universities Press.

Preface

Freud's writings on sadomasochism (1905, 1911, 1919, 1920, 1924) tell us that sadism and masochism are closely enmeshed as manifestations of the aggressive instinct, with one or the other coming to the fore. Brenner (1959) addresses himself to the complexity involved in simultaneously viewing sadism and masochism in the same person. He states:

> It is no surprise to be told by one author that the unconscious mechanism behind a masochistic patient's behavior is one of mollifying his parent and winning his love by submission to him, and to learn from another author that such

behavior represents an unconscious fantasy of humiliating and triumphing over one's parent. On the contrary, one expects there will be both a sadistic and masochistic, both a submissive and aggressive meaning to every patient's masochism. Each has defensive functions as well as being a means of instinctual gratification. (p. 210)

Viewing sadism and masochism as simultaneous and opposite seems to be the bias of the author intent on remaining within the rubric of traditional drive theory. In an overview of the concept of aggression Brenner (1972) tells us that the validity of the death drive is a matter for biologists to decide; the question of its validity does not affect Freud's assumption that aggression is an instinctual drive in man's mental life. Stone (1971), an equally well known Freudian theoretician, holds the opposite viewpoint. He suggests that the reasons for aggression are diverse enough to raise serious doubts about it being an instinctual drive. Stone perceives aggression as a drive to master traumatic helplessness, whether actual or threatened.

It seems the rule to overlook the vast inequality between child and parent. To the young child the parent is everything; survival literally depends on the parent's sustained physical and emotional nurturance. During this period of "pleasureable obedience" (Ferenzi 1909) parents and/or their surrogates may be viewed as omniscient or they may be overglorified. If these idealized figures behave ambivalently or even fallibly, the infant may introject them as demons or witches. A masochistic paradigm is actually more typical of the prolonged dependency of childhood than a sadistic one, despite the sadistic psychosexual behavior usually attributed to the developmental aspects of the child's oral, anal, phallic, and genital phases. Anna Freud (1965), for example, correlates biting, spitting, and devouring with orality; sadistic torturing, hitting, kicking, and destroying with anality; over-bearing, domineering, and forceful behavior with the phallic phase; and antisocial outbursts with adolescence.

The masochistic individual frequently exhibits a need for drama, crisis, sensation, stimulation, heightened tension, abandonment to misery, and self-degradation, which brings about a spurious sense of vitality. Genuine or autonomous feelings are frequently muted, and life is experienced as occurring outside of the individual's control, not to be responded to, but to be reacted to submissively, sometimes blindly. An oppositional relationship may help maintain a desirable state of extreme tension. An antagonistic relationship may be more tolerable than a positive one or none at all. In a recent evaluation of current concepts in masochism, Fischer (1981) suggests that the individual achieves gratifying self-definition, establishes self boundaries, and defends against the dangers and anxieties associated with identity diffusion through self-induced physical pain.

Masochistic transference resistances do not necessarily lead to negative therapeutic reactions or failures despite Freud's assertions to the contrary (1937). The literature on this topic (Olinick 1970, Sandler 1973) suggests varied inter-pretations and ameliorative therapeutic procedures. It is arbitrary to deflect responsibility for therapeutic impasses onto the patient. More realistically, analysis is a reciprocal, collaborative relationship with mutual tasks unique for each member of the analytic dyad. The analyst must be aware that the therapeutic relationship is imbalanced by the arrange-ments and appurtenances of the analytic format (Menaker 1942, Stone 1961). The global attitudes of the analyst, includ-ing the quality of his or her countertransference and affirma-tiveness and commitment regarding the patient, are as deci-sive in affecting the course of therapy as the patient's communications, transferences, and resistances. Each instance of stasis or impasse must be examined with reference to dynamic and genetic stages of the "motivational hierarchy" (Brenman 1952) of sadomasochistic behavior. One could also view the masochistic transference reaction as an avoidance of separation, a lack of readiness to resolve the separation-individuation dilemma, or a developmental need for the prolonged empathic climate provided by the therapeutic relationship. This relationship is clearly decisive in the patient's gradual metamorphosis.

The traditional explanations of masochism that have been proffered are clinging to illness, need for punishment concerning unconscious incestuous guilt, and the death instinct. More recent studies have emphasized "defensive flight from castration anxiety" (Spiegel 1978), wherein castration anxiety is avoided by bringing the latent anxiety and accompanying rage to the patient's attention before masochistic formations appear. As castration anxiety is worked through, the superego becomes more integrated, and the result is "anticipatory guilt" rather than "futile remorse."

In the "masochistic contract" (Smirnoff 1969) the masochist appears as an educator rather than the "victimized accomplice to a sadistic executioner," just as the sadist is the "pedagogue of his reluctant victim." According to Smirnoff, masochism must be redefined as the "actualization of a contract which must regulate the relationship in the masochistic performance."

The double-mask defense (Grand 1973) occurs when the individual feels insubstantial and wishes to give an illusion of adult competence. He wishes for a parental overseer rather than to acquire a sense of mastery for himself.

Blum (1976) suggests that, contrary to the literature on female masochism, there is no evidence that women have a greater propensity than men to derive pleasure from pain or that they possess a lesser capacity for neutralization and secondary autonomy.

Stolorow and Lachmann (1980) emphasize that the confluence of masochistic and narcissistic components in sadistic individuals points to an early, massive disappointment in, or absence of, the idealized primary object, followed by a fixation on the primitive, grandiose self to restore the damaged self-concept. One wonders, in view of such early traumatization, how there is a grandiose self to be found at all.

In Fromm's overview of destructive-sadistic modalities (1973), sadistic individuals seek total control over others, are intent on self-aggrandizement and the acquisition of power, live aggressively through others, and hope to destroy or exploit their partners. In this context sadism is prompted by a sense of emotional impotence; the desire for power over others compensates for the incapacity to create or love.

In delineating the sadomasochistic character, Kernberg (1976) indicates an early history of extreme frustration and aggression. He alludes to a sense of triumph in the power of self-destructiveness as well as enjoyment in the suffering and defeat of others, which he relates to oral envy. Such individuals lack a well-integrated superego and the capacity to experience guilt or concern. They resort to splitting as a central defense, expressed by alternating, contradictory ego states. Their dissociation is reinforced by denial, primitive idealization, omnipotence, and projective identification.

Masochistic and sadistic formations are interpersonal interactions where intrapsychic dynamics concerning the self and characterological structures concerning the elaboration of assertion and control differ for each partner. Perhaps the polarity of dominance and submission might better describe expectable power operations, given the texture of our culture. Globally sadistic individuals rarely seek treatment or acknowledge any subjective disturbance at all. Perhaps this is the reason masochistic paradigms have been more thoroughly investigated by Freud and others. Sadistic-destructive personality structures do exist, however. Megalomaniacal leaders have sought to transform the world to fulfill their personal needs. They have sought to annihilate all opponents and have altered reality to suit their "malignant narcissism."

REFERENCES

Blum, H. P. (1976), Masochism, the ego ideal and the psychology of women. *J. Am. Psychoanal. Assoc.*, 24: 157–193.

Brenman, M. (1952), On teasing and being teased and the problems of "moral masochism." In *The Psychoanalytic Study of the Child*, 7: 264–285. New York: International Universities Press.

Brenner, C. (1959), The masochistic character. *J. Am. Psychoanal. Assoc.*, 7: 197–226.

_____ (1972), The psychoanalytic concept of aggression. *Int. J. Psychoanal.*, 52: 137–144.

Fischer, N. (1981), Masochism: current concepts. *J. Am. Psychoanal. Assoc.*, 29: 673–688.

Freud, S. (1905), *Three Essays on the Theory of Sexuality*. New York: Nervous and Mental Disease Monographs.

_____ (1911), Formulations regarding the two principles in mental functioning. In *Collected Papers*, 4: 13–22. London: Hogarth Press.

_____ (1919), A child is being beaten. A Contribution to the study of the origin of sexual perversions. In *Collected Papers*, 2: 172–201. London: Hogarth Press.

_____ (1920), *Beyond the Pleasure Principle*. London: Hogarth Press.

_____ (1924), The economic problem in masochism. In *Collected Papers*, 2: 255–268. London: Hogarth Press.

_____ (1937), Analysis terminable and interminable. In *Collected Papers*, 5: 316–357. London: Hogarth Press.

Fromm, E. (1973), *Anatomy of Human Destructiveness.* New York: Holt, Rinehart and Winston.

Grand, H. (1973), The masochistic defense of the 'double mask.' *Int. J. Psychoanal.*, 54: 445–454.

Kernberg, O. (1976), *Borderline Conditions and Pathological Narcissism.* New York: Aronson.

Kohut, H. (1977), *The Restoration of the Self.* New York: International Universities Press.

Menaker, E. (1942), The masochistic factor in the psychoanalytic situation. *Psychoanal. Q.*, 11: 171–186.

Olinick, S. (1970), Panel report. Negative therapeutic reaction. *J. Am. Psychoanal. Assoc.*, 18: 655–672.

Sandler, J., Dare, C., and Holder, D. (1973), *The Patient and the Analyst.* New York: International Universities Press.

Smirnoff, V. (1969), The masochistic contract. *Int. J. Psychoanal.*, 50: 655–671.

Spiegel, L. (1978), Moral masochism. *Psychoanal. Q.*, 47: 209–236.

Stolorow, R. D. and Lachmann, F. (1980), *Psychoanalysis and Developmental Arrests.* New York: International Universities Press.

Stone, L. (1961), *The Psychoanalytic Situation.* New York: International Univerities Press.

_____ (1971), Reflections on the psychoanaltyic concept of aggression. *Psychoanal. Q.*, 40: 195–244.

Acknowledgments

I would like to thank Doctors Gerard Chrzanowski, Alan Roland, Benjamin Brody, Samuel Dunkell, and Anna Antonovsky for their infinitely helpful evaluations of my manuscript; Dr. Jason Aronson for his excellent suggestions for the enrichment of my material and his general encouragement and nurturance; the editors and staff of Jason Aronson, Inc., for their exemplary efforts; and my patients for their willingness to share their struggles and aspirations.

I. Introduction

Masochism, a singularly important element in human behavior, has long been the subject of psychoanalytic enquiry as well as controversy. Initially viewed by Krafft-Ebing (1900) solely in terms of sexual perversion, masochism was perceived by Freud to be an essentially instinctual or biological phenomenon. Later psychoanalytic investigators have sought its motivational source in cultural conditions or explored its workings in terms of defensive, adaptive, and even normal human behavior.

Whatever concept of masochism is postulated, it is evident that masochistic phenomena provide a disturbing accompaniment to innumerable aspects of human action and cultural forms. The Christian ethic has sanctified masochism in such religious practices as mortification and its most extreme variant, asceticism. Masochism has been institutionalized in the personal and mass desolation of warfare, passively endured. Its elements can be seen in the tenets of medieval court chivalry, where "courtesy" demanded complete acceptance of the unattainability of the female and an adherence to those elaborate rituals of unrequited love that are so clearly the precursors of modern ideas of romantic love. It is further evidenced in the morbid, necrophiliac torrents of the romantic movement's exalted lyrics. Finally masochism seems to be inherent in the very texture of Western civilization and its political structure: Our social origins appear to lie in the fact that some groups of men are willing to submit to other groups who hold the keys of power, a societal germ that finds its full flowering in fascist ideology.

As a psychological concept, masochism was first considered by Krafft-Ebing. In his investigation of deviant sexual behavior, he described masochism as a perversion in which erotic pleasure is obtained from the passive acquiescence to—or even seeking out of—brutal and humiliating responses from another. The term had been culled from the name of the Austrian writer, Leopold von Sacher-Masoch, whose life and writings illuminate this characteristic with exemplary fullness. *Venus in Furs* (1870), Sacher-Masoch's most widely read novel, is replete with florid details of the manipulation, torture, and subjugation of the "hero" by a voluptuous, but icy, tormentress clothed in full regalia of furs, boots, and whip.

Sadism, also described by Krafft-Ebing, is defined as a sexual perversion in which pleasure is derived by assuming the role of active donor of pain and inflicting this on others in the form of beatings or humiliation. The Marquis de Sade, whose writings display an ingenious and flamboyant interplay of lust and cruelty, gives his name to this concept.

According to Krafft-Ebing, pain—exaggerated or artificially induced—can intensify sexual stimulation in the event that normal sexual responses do not effect gratification. He asserts, furthermore, that the concept of "sexual bondage," presumably less prevalent in men than in women, best explains masochism:

> When the idea of being tyrannized is for a long time closely associated with the lustful thought of the beloved person, the lustful emotion is finally, transferred to the tyranny itself, and the transformation to perversion is completed. This is the manner in which masochism may be acquired by cultivation.

When masochistic behavior appears deep-seated and is evidenced in childhood, it is believed by Krafft-Ebing, in accordance with the thinking of his time, to be congenital.

In his early writings on the topic, Freud considered masochistic formations to be a unique mixture of pain and pleasure, with their source in the tendency of infants to respond to increases in psychic tension with "sexual excitement." Painful tensions, Freud thought, could also elicit concomitant sexual responses in infancy, thus providing the physiological basis for "erogenous masochism," substrate of all other species of masochism.

Furthermore, according to Freud, "active and passive forms" of masochism typically occur in the same individual. Masochism is, in essence, one's own sadism turned round upon itself. Masochistic fantasies have to do with psychic conflicts inhering in the oedipal period, focusing on the role of guilt, castration anxiety, and need for punishment. In addition, masochism, or the desire to be beaten, appears as a regressive or "anal" substitute for incestuous wishes regarding the parent (Freud, 1919). Later, Freud (1920, 1923) postulated two forces of equal impact, the life and death instincts, that are in constant interaction with one another and in various states of fusion or defusion.

Freud's seminal theories on masochism were considerably in advance of previous writers. However, he did not pay sufficient attention to the possible origin of masochistic attitudes in the vicissitudes of the early mother–child attachment. Many of Freud's formulations seem limited because he neglected to elaborate or discuss nuances of the various aspects of oedipal interactions, especially the full implications of the parents' primary participation in, or catalyzing of, the oedipal situation. Finally, when he came to formulate his ultimate theory on masochism, he was already in the grips of the Thanatos concept that colored all his last postulates and transformed his early, open-ended and exploratory approach into a narrow and circumscribed one.

Insofar as the contemporary concept of masochistic behavior is concerned, what would be most meaningful is a construct focusing on mother–child, as well as oedipal, interactions and encompassing the individual's development throughout infancy, childhood, and beyond in his total intra- and interfamilial setting. In such a framework, where both genetic and developmental factors play a role, masochism and sadism are most validly perceived not as necessarily occurring intrapsychically, but as interrelational reciprocities. Here intrapsychic dynamics and character structure, especially in regard to the nuances of aggression, differ for each partner.

In exploring the vast literature on masochism, both Freudian and post-Freudian, the areas that demand most attention because of past controversy or neglect may be subsumed in the following questions:

1. What are the unique characteristics in the individual's life history, particularly in the parent–child and family constellation, that make imperative the recourse to masochistic behavior?
2. What are the techniques employed by masochistic personalities for coping with aggression? Is the masochist both sadist and sufferer, that is, sadomasochistic? Or, is this a misleading merging of two distinct entities?
3. How do masochistic mechanisms differ from depressive, obsessional or paranoid patterns of behavior, often confused with aspects of masochistic suffering?
4. What is meant by the merging of pain and pleasure, that is, the "joy of suffering"?

Before delving into these questions in Chapters V–VIII, a systematic overview of Freud's theories on masochism will be attempted in Chapter II to provide frame of reference and context. Further contributions to the literature on masochism, a rich and by now monumental one, will be summarized in Chapter III, to be followed by clinical illustrations in Chapter IV.

II. Freud's Evolving Theories on Masochism

In a series of clinical and theoretical papers, Freud undertook to explore the meaning of masochism. *Three Contributions to the Theory of Sex* (1905), his earliest investigation of the topic of masochism provides a discussion of sexual aberrations and amplifies Krafft-Ebing's theories. With reference to sexual perversion, Freud singled out as most significant the "desire to inflict pain on another." Though other writers have preferred to focus on algolagnia, thereby underlining the pleasure in pain and cruelty, the concepts chosen by Krafft-Ebing that Freud adhered to, emphasize rather the pleasure accompanying any form of humiliation or subjection. Active algolagnia or sadism is attributed to a "normal, aggressive component in the sexual impulse of man." Should sexual gratification be solely sought by over-powering or devaluing the partner, one can more strictly consider this behavior perversion. Masochism, according to Freud, represents the totality of passive attitudes subsumed in sexual behavior. Its "extreme" form indicates that satisfaction is connected with physical or mental suffering in regard to the sexual partner. Masochism as a perversion is considered by Freud to be further removed from the "normal" sexual goal than its opposite, sadism.

Masochism is sadism turned round upon the self, which serves as surrogate for the sexual partner. Exaggerated instances of masochistic perversion show that factors such as castration complex and sense of guilt intensify and fixate the original, passive sexual attitude.

In addition, Freud asserts that the history of civilization reveals a correlation between cruelty and sexual instinct, perhaps a "relic of cannibalistic desires." He points out that perversions often occur in "contrasting pairs" and that pain always conjures up feelings of pleasure. The most conspicuous aspect of the sadomasochistic perversion is that active and passive forms are habitually found to occur together in the same individual. One who feels pleasure in evoking pain in his sexual partner may also find pleasurable any pain that he may himself derive from sexual relations. The sadist is simultaneously a masochist; active or passive aspects of the perversion may come to the fore, representing one's prevailing sexual activity. The pair of opposites formed by sadism and masochism cannot be attributed "merely to aggressiveness" but are related to the "united contrast of male and female in bisexuality, replaced in psychoanalysis by the contrast between activity and passivity."

Freud also notes that the "cruelty component" of the

sexual drive is quite marked in the pregenital organization of children inasmuch as the capacity for sympathy develops comparatively late.[1]

In his essay "On the Sexual Theories of Children," germane to, though not specifically dealing with masochism, Freud (1908) indicated that the child harbors a fairly sadistic conception of sexual intercourse, one wherein the female is assulted, mistreated, or humiliated by the male.

Freud (1915a) also pointed out that, for some, the promise of success may arouse motives that can be gratified only through failure. This refers to individuals who become emotionally ill on the advent of a long cherished, deeply rooted wish or aspiration, as though they could not "endure their bliss." Freud links this to rearousal of oedipal conflicts, to fear of superseding the father.

"Instincts and Their Vicissitudes" (Freud, 1915b), comprising a further elaboration of the concept of masochism, states that all instincts evidence transformations such as "reversal into its opposite" or "turning round upon the subject," though this phenomenon is particularly found in polarities such as sadism and masochism. The reversal involves a change from actice to passive, from torturing to being tortured. A reversal of content such as love into hate is revealed as well. "Turning round" of the instinct indicates the following sequence: Initially the person or "subject" behaves aggressively towards another individual or "object." The object (without elaboration as to motivational nuance) is abandoned and replaced by the subject, that is, one directs the aggression against oneself. Ultimately still another person is sought as object to assume one's original, sadistic role. Freud introduces Bleuler's term "ambivalence"

[1] Murphy and Murphy (1937) found evidence of sympathy in two-year-olds, in some when "secure and happy," in others when "troubles heighten their awareness of the needs of others."

to describe the linking of a primary instinct with its passive opposite. He feels the degree of demonstrable ambivalence varies considerably in individuals, groups, and races.

After the transformation into masochism has occurred, the experience of pain, serves as a "passive masochistic aim." Pain is linked to sexual excitation with its concomitant pleasurable effects, so that the person "gladly" pursues the unpleasantness of pain. Should a particular configuration of pain be experienced in context of a "passive masochistic aim," one may again switch back to the sadistic aim of inflicting pain, simultaneously and masochistically deriving pleasure via this identification with the suffering object. In either instance it is not the pain that is enjoyed but the accompanying sexual excitement.

In Freud's next paper on the subject of masochism, "A Child Is Being Beaten: A Contribution to the Study of the Origin of Sexual Perversions" (1919), he noted the frequency with which the masturbatory fantasy "a child is being beaten" occurred in those individuals with diagnoses of hysteria and obsessional neurosis; this fantasy is acknowledged by his patients with considerable uncertainty and resistance and is accompanied by a sense of shame and guilt.

After establishing the fact that his patients' fantasies probably took place before ages five to six, it became apparent to Freud that the fantasies were reinforced or conjured up by witnessing the punishment of classmates by one's teacher. At a later age the fantasies were prompted by reading such novels as *Uncle Tom's Cabin*, or the child himself produced a multitude of fantasies in which other children were beaten or disciplined for naughtiness or "bad" behavior.

In working with several female patients, Freud's intensive analyses of their beating fantasies indicated that the latter were transformed in various ways with respect to their connection to the author of the fantasy, their object, content, and significance. The initial phase of the fantasy focuses on a quite early stage of childhood, hence the indefiniteness of its elaboration.

The child enduring the beating is never the author of the fantasy but is usually a sibling. The figure performing the punishment is an adult, at first ambiguous as to identity though later recognized as father: "My father is beating the child" designates the first phase. At this stage the fantasy is not yet truly masochistic, relates Freud; nor is it sadistic, since the child creating the fantasy is not performing the beating.

Considerable transformation occurs between this first phase and the next. The person administering the beating remains constant, but the child who is the recipient of the beating is now the child producing the fantasy. Moreover, the fantasy, accompanied by a "high degree of pleasure" now has as content: "I am being beaten by my father," displaying "unmistakably" masochistic features. This second phase is most crucial, though, as Freud says: "It has never had a real existence. It is never remembered, has never succeeded in becoming conscious. It is a construction of analysis. . . ."

In the third phase, as in the first, the person performing the beating is not father but a father-surrogate or authority figure, usually a teacher. The child producing the fantasy is no longer present but is merely a spectator. Nor is it one child being beaten but several, generally boys, unknown to the person. The beating, formerly fairly clear cut, may now appear complicated in that punishments and humiliations of various sorts may be substituted for the beating itself. Distinguishing this phase is the sexual excitement attached to the fantasy, eventuating in masturbation.

Exploring the successive stages of the fantasy, Freud

felt the first phase represented the incestuous, as well as sibling rivalry attitudes of the child: "Father loves only me and not the other child because he is beating him." The fantasy

> gratifies the child's jealousy and is dependent upon the erotic side of his life, but it is also powerfully reinforced by its egoistic interest. It remains doubtful whether it ought to be described as purely sexual, nor can one venture to call it sadistic.

As repression proceeds, however, prompted by the birth of a sibling—this, in turn, experienced as faithlessness on father's part and reinforced by unexpected slights—a sense of guilt emerges, reversing the preceding process: "No, he does not love you, for he is beating you." The fantasy of the second phase, that of being beaten by father, is a direct expression of the sense of guilt to which the love for father is subordinated, transforming sadism into masochism. Entirely unconscious, the fantasy represents a regression to the pregenital, anal–sadistic organization of sexual life; that is, it is not only punishment for the forbidden, genital relationship but the regressive substitute for it. From this latter source it derives the "libidinal excitation which is from this time forward attached to it and which finds its outlet in onanistic acts, the essence of masochism."

In the third phase the fantasy "father is beating the other child, he loves only me," is sadistic, though the gratification derived is masochistic, according to Freud. Its importance, he states, "lies in the fact that it has taken over the libidinal cathexis of the repressed portion and at the same time the sense of guilt which is attached to its content." The children being beaten by teacher, invariably boys, are surrogates for the child. Girls, in turning away from their incestuous love for father, are now susceptible to the "masculinity complex" and wish to be boys.

The beating fantasy occurs with reference to boys in the event that a negative, oedipal wish sexualizes the thought of being beaten by father. Masochistic men thus supplant the unconscious idea of a beating by father with the less objectionable one of a beating by a woman, as a substitute for mother.

In a highly theoretical and speculative paper, "Beyond the Pleasure Principle," perhaps prompted by his lifelong preoccupation with death, Freud (1920) formulated his celebrated concept of the "death instinct," that is, his conclusion that the fundamental aim of all instincts is the wish to revert to an earlier state. Inasmuch as instincts aimed at the past, why should they stop, asked Freud, before reducing a living organism to a prevital state, that of inorganic matter. This presumably represents an inertia in organic life, a tendency to restore an earlier state "to its logical conclusion." Freud noted that while consideration of the repetition-compulsion (equating the tendency to repetition with that of restoring a previous state of affairs) was the first motive for promulgating a death instinct, it was the stability or constancy principle that suggested the strongest argument for it. According to the constancy principle the essential function of mental activity consists in reducing to as low a level as possible the tensions induced by either instinctual or external excitation.

Freud suggested that the repetition compulsion goes beyond the pleasure principle. He was alluding here to the fondness of children for repeating games or stories whether or not they are pleasurable; to recurrent dreams of war neurotics in which the original trauma is revived again and again; to the pattern of self-injuring behavior pervasive in the lives of some; and to the tendency of many patients during psychoanalysis to act out over and over unpleasant experiences of their childhood.

In order to avoid a monistic view of life—for example, that the ultimate aim of life leads to death—Freud pointed out that though the sexual instincts reinstated earlier forms of being and therefore became part of the death instinct, their mode of action had the merit of indefinitely postponing the final goal of the death instinct. By so doing, by creating new life, the sexual instincts thwarted or diverted the aim of the death instinct and could be viewed as counterposed to it. Freud thus succeeded in establishing two opposing forces in the mind, life and death instincts, each of equal validity and status and in constant struggle with one another.

Previously, Freud pointed to a primary, aggressive or destructive instinct that, when fused with sexual impulses, eventuated in the perversion sadism, in turn part of the ego instincts. Masochism was considered the opposite of sadism, that is, sadism turned round against the self. In "Beyond the Pleasure Principle" Freud reversed the sequence, and suggested that there could be a primary masochism, a self-injuring tendency from which destructive and sadistic impulses could be derived. Sadistic behavior that cannot be channeled into the environment may then be directed against the self, producing a secondary masochism superimposed onto the primary kind. Sexual or life instincts seek to hold onto or prolong life by diverting the self-destructive tendencies outward against others, implying a perpetual oscillation between man's instinct for survival and his relentless urge to reinstate his former inorganic self.

In *The Ego and the Id*, a book introducing the concept of the superego (1923), Freud postulated that the more intense the Oedipus complex and the more effectively it is repressed due to cumulative effects of discipline, religion and schooling, the more exacting and dominating will the superego, in the guise of conscience or an unconscious sense of guilt, be over the ego. The differentiation of superego from ego emerges as one of the most significant events in the development of the individual and the race: "By giving indelible representation to the influence of the parents, the existence of factors having to do with its origin is perpetuated." The superego, an extension of the concept of ego ideal (Freud, 1914; 1922), delineates the deficiencies of the actual self and assists the self in attaining stricter standards in the moral or aesthetic sphere. The superego is closely interwoven with a profound sense of guilt, and its activity is eased by suffering or punishment.

The superego may propel the individual to punish himself without knowing why he does so. The greater control exerted by the individual over his aggressive impulses, the more tyrranical does the superego apparently become. In addition, the superego is considered close to the id, so that a part of the sense of guilt is unconscious, since the conscience is closely connected with the vicissitudes of the Oedipus complex.

Perhaps the most salient feature of the superego is its cruelty and relentlessness, particularly noted in depressed patients and in patients with obsessional neuroses.

"The Economic Problem in Masochism" (Freud, 1924) differentiates "erotogenic" from "feminine" masochism. In addition, a "moral" category of masochism is introduced. Erotogenic masochism, the "lust of pain," is also found as substrate of the other forms. Moral masochism, perhaps the "most important form" in which masochism is manifested, "has only lately, as a sense of guilt that is for the most part unconscious, been properly appreciated by psychoanalysis." Feminine masochism is the form most accessible to observation.

In feminine masochism (in men), the fantasies that lead to masturbation, constitute sexual gratification, or induce potency, have to do with situations in which one is bound, beaten, forced to obey unconditionally, or degraded. Freud suggested that the masochist longs to be regarded as a small, helpless, dependent, especially naughty child: He may identify with a feminine role, inasmuch as he fantasies he is castrated; assumes the passive role in coitus; or feels he is participating in giving birth. Masochistic tortures, according to Freud, are qualitatively different from the brutalities, fantasied or actual, of sadists. Rarely, for example, does the thought of mutilation occur in their content. Feelings of guilt emerge in regard to the manifest content of masochistic fantasies almost as though the individual had committed a crime, perhaps related to infantile masturbation, that he seeks to expiate by subjecting himself to pain and torture.

Erotogenic masochism is explained in the following way: Presumably, both the concepts death instinct and primal sadism are identical with masochism. After the sadistic components have been directed outwards towards objects, the "true" erotogenic masochism remains as a residue within the organism, on the one hand becoming a component of the libido, and on the other preserving the individual himself as object. Thus, "this masochism would be a witness and a survival of that phase of development in which the amalagamation . . . of death instinct and Eros took place." The erotogenic form evolves through the psychosexual developmental stages of the libido. Fear of being devoured by the totem animal or father stems from the early oral stage, while the desire to be beaten by father evolves from the following, anal–sadistic period. Castration anxiety, though subsequently denied, enters into the content of masochistic fantasies as residue of the phallic stage, and from the final, genital stage situations characteristic of female development emerge, as, for example, the passive role in coitus, as well as the act of giving birth.

In moral masochism it is the suffering or self-injury that is stressed, no matter who inflicts it, person or fate. Freud traced moral masochism to an unconscious sense of guilt or "need for punishment." Also, moral masochists, characterized in the analytic situation by their "negative therapeutic reaction," are among those manifesting "one of the most difficult resistances and the greatest menace to the success of our medical or educative aims." Gratification of the previously mentioned unconscious sense of guilt is perhaps the strongest component in what is termed the "advantage through illness." Forces opposed to resolving the neurosis, that is, the sufferings inherent in the neurosis, are of decisive value to the masochistic trend. Moral masochists are "dominated by an especially sensitive conscience, although they are not at all conscious of any such ultra-morality. . . ."

Freud postulates a distinction between moral masochism and unconscious development of morality. In the latter, the stress is on the heightened sadism of the superego to which the ego submits; in the former, the emphasis is on the masochistic ego seeking punishment either from the superego or from the parental figures. In both there is a desire for punishment and suffering, as well as an intimate relationship between ego and superego. The sadism of the superego is, for the most part, perceived consciously, while the masochistic impulse of the ego remains concealed from the person and can only be inferred from his behavioral patterns.

Freud points out that unconscious feelings of guilt indicate a need for punishment by the parental authority. In turn, the wish to be beaten by father is connected with passive, sexual aims regarding him, representing a regressive distortion of the latter. Conscience and morality have to do with resolution or "desexualizing" of the Oedipus complex. In moral masochism, morality is sexualized, that is, the Oedipus complex is revived, and a regression from morality back to the Oedipus complex ensues. One may salvage some degree of morality concomitant to one's masochism, yet one's conscience may then become enveloped by one's masochism. One's masochism may set up a predilection towards "sinful acts" that can only be absolved by the accusations of the "sadistic conscience [as in so many Russian character-types] or by chastisement from the great parental authority of Fate." To elicit punishment from Fate "the masochist must do something inexpedient, act against his own best interests, ruin the prospects which the real world offers him, and possibly destroy his own existence in the world of reality."

Freud stated his failure to isolate what he termed the "genesis" of masochism. This may be attributed in part to his ultimate and inexorable emphasis on instinctual causation, which snuffed out any further delving into the nuances of masochism and, more basically, to his disinclination to look for the origin of masochistic attitudes in the substrate of the early, pre-oedipal, mother–child relationship. Of course, Freud's nuclear theories, the oedipal and psychosexual, take into account the role of parent or "object," but Freud emphasized the inevitability of each phase, rather than the possibility of a unique emergent emanating from a particular set of life experiences.

The farthest Freud permitted himself to reflect along more dynamic lines appeared in his paper, "A Child Is Being Beaten" (1919), where he indicates that people who harbor beating fantasies develop a special sensitivity and irritability towards any one whom they view as a father figure: "They allow themselves to be easily offended by a person of this kind, and in that way . . . bring about the realization of the imagined situation of being beaten by their father." In a succeeding paper, Freud (1924) negated this insight, however, by stating that though "to all other masochistic sufferings there still clings the condition that it should be administered by the loved person . . . in the moral type of masochism . . . it is the suffering itself that matters," disregarding the object. Contradictorily, Freud, in the same paper, concludes that the self-beratement and guilt of the moral masochist has to do with disguised sexual wishes regarding the father.

One would hazard the notion that the beating fantasies described by Freud's female patients represented not only a covert, incestuous wish for the patriarchal father but also a perception of an unpredictable, implacable, as well as seductive, father, eventuating in masochistic expectations regarding him. Also, the child's view of the mother's attitudes regarding sexual and feminine roles, as well as the child's perception of the total relationship between the parents, might point to the father as distant or assaultive, and the mother as martyred and victimized. The child might further be receptive to masochistic interactions based on previous, noxious experiences with the mother. A more workable view of the etiology of masochism would envisage the child in his total familial setting; focus on the early or preoedipal interrelationships of mother and child; externalize the constellation of parental ambivalence throughout each of the developmental phases, and beyond; encompass the father's role, usually undelineated, in the entire family structure, the early relationship with father, and the vicissitudes of the oedipal and later phases; consider the relationship between parents and with siblings; and evaluate constitutional predispositions, i.e., intensity of the child's needs, as well as characteristic responses to frustration.

Freud's views regarding the centrality of the oedipal phase in the development of masochistic patterns appeared subsequently to be displaced or supplemented by explorations concerning the importance of the earlier, mother–child relationship. Oral disappointments intruding on the feelings of so-called infantile omnipotence were later seen as the more crucial component in masochism. Freud (1933) himself eventually acknowledged a belated recognition of the preoedipal attachment to mother, its intensity, and central role in the child's development.

III. Further Contributions
to the Literature on Masochism

ON THE DEATH INSTINCT

Students of Freud dwelt within his framework, though adherence to Thanatos as an explanation of masochistic behavior was not widespread. Alexander (1924), however, clings to the death instinct theory to explain neurosis: "The primary disease process is a turning of the death instinct against one's own self in the form of an over-severity of the superego." Menninger (1938) assumes that the life and death instincts are in constant conflict and interaction, comparable to similar forces in physics, chemistry, and biology:

"To create and to destroy, to build up and tear down, are the anabolism and katabolism of the personality. . . ." These forces originally turned inward are eventually directed toward other objects, in consonance with one's physical growth and personality maturation. Failure to accomplish this results in a continuum of self-destructive behavior.

Melanie Klein (1940) also accepts Freud's dual instinct theory. Indeed, she asserts that the aggressive or sadistic drive emerges at birth or shortly thereafter and suggests that excessive frustration facilitates projection of sadistic fantasies onto the mother figure. Fearful of retaliation, the infant adheres to the "paranoid position" where persecutory anxiety prevails. The "depressive position" subsequently emerges, consonant with the wish to preserve the good mother or to restore her after the infant has "destroyed" her; at this phase both libidinal and aggressive wishes are prevalent. Inasmuch as the aggressive drive has been accelerated to such a degree, even good mothering cannot prevent the occurrence of the two stages though modulation of their impact may occur.

Nunberg (1955) regards the infant's biting of fingers or toes as evidence of primal masochism, embodying the earliest manifestation of the death instinct. He distinguishes between this primal masochism and "actual" masochism, where the death instinct fuses with narcissistic libido.

Waelder (1964) also accepts the death instinct theory but maintains a more moderate view. He differentiates "reactive" and "essential" destructiveness: The former is elicited by threats to ambition or self-preservation or by frustration of libidinal impulses and may include aggressive by-products of the individual's attempts to control his own body and master the external world. "Reactive" aggression may also form part of the libidinal drive as noted in incorporation and penetration fantasies. "Essential" destructiveness is attributed to the death instinct as, for example, in situations where aggression is "deeply rooted" in the individual or as seen in psychotic acts of murder and suicide.

Most psychoanalysts, however, reject the metaphysical notions of the death instinct. Though Fenichel (1935) acknowledges the importance and existence of aggressive drives, he takes issue with Freud's assertion that they always and necessarily emerge as a turning outward of more primary, self-destructive drives. Also, he questions Freud's notion that on archaic levels death and ego instincts are "defused" and that they fuse gradually during maturation, Eros neutralizing the death instinct. Rather he postulates a common matrix from which Eros and aggression are later differentiated.

Hartmann *et al.* (1949) formulate a theory of aggression as an independent instinct. Libido and aggression, they believe, may be compared as to source, nature of discharge, and aims. Certain organ zones are the source of both stimulation and gratification of libido, but aggression is not zone-specific as to source or gratification, and the zones involved in discharge involve widespread musculature. Aggressive discharge is less structured than libidinal discharge, but there are elements of fore-pleasure and satisfaction in aggressive, as well as in sexual behavior. While the aims of sexuality are diversified, the aims of aggression are rigid and narrow. However, the plasticity of aggression is seen in the variety of means it can utilize to attain satisfaction.

Psychoanalytic ego psychology assumed a crucial role in restructuring the many-leveled implications of the aggressive drive. Hartmann (1964) indicated that the aggressive drive may be neutralized and that different human endeavors necessitate variegated patterns of neutralization. Should neutralization occur, aggression may be transformed into assertion, work, or mastery of the environment.

Countering Freud's death instinct theory, psychoanalytic ego psychology no longer perceived the aggressive drive as embodying a desire to return to inorganic life but rather as a crucial life force. In addition, in Hartmann's view (1964):

> Aggressive energy participates in the development of psychic structure, but the psychic systems, once they are formed also provide it with specific modes of expression. Reality situations in man appeal sometimes to the unmitigated expression of aggression, but in many more cases to its sublimation.

More currently, Stone (1971) challenges the notion that aggression is a primary instinctual drive, stating that "aggression arises in the drive to master actual or threatened traumatic helplessness."

ON FEMININE MASOCHISM

To Freud (1924) masochism seemed "truly feminine": Feminine masochism has to do with repression of aggressiveness, enjoined on women by their "constitutions and by society."

Horney (1939) is convinced that masochistic phenomena in women are not primarily found in the sexual realm but represent conflicts in interpersonal relationships, as well as attempts to gain safety and satisfaction in life through inconspicuousness, oblivion, and "ecstatic abandonment to misery and self-degradation." The core of masochistic formations has to do with "the attempt of an intimidated individual to cope with life and its dangers by dependency and unobtrusiveness."

Annie Reich's paper on "Extreme Submissiveness in Women" (1940) cites the tendency of women to fall in love with men who abuse and humiliate them. They consider intercourse an act of violence; or the act may be perceived as a "mystic dissolution of the person which has its climax in death during orgasm." The humiliations to which the submissive woman acquiesces are a part of the love ritual; the greater the unhappiness over abuse or separation, the greater the joy of reunion. Reich indicates that there are two parts in the scenario: that which is destroyed in the first part is restored in the second.

As noted in the dream of her patient—"a father operates on the penis of a little boy; then he loves the boy very much"—the woman has first to be castrated and destroyed by the man in order to be loved afterward. Reich further suggests that analysis of the submissive woman evidences that her problems precede the phallic period, i.e., they are attributable to a "childish" fixation on mother. Desires originally focused on the mother—protection, tenderness, and food—reappear in an ecstatic love relationship to a man.

Helene Deutsch (1944) indicates that in women the entire psychological preparation for the sexual act is replete with masochistic implications. Coitus is closely connected with the act of defloration, rape, painful penetration, even the destruction of a part of the body. Masochistic attitudes accompany the reproductive functions as well. Conscious and unconscious fantasies relating to childbirth in all its phases have a "painful and dangerous character" throughout. Emotional aspects of the "female castration complex," in addition to components of the menstrual process, also contribute to feminine masochism.

Fenichel (1945) suggests that extreme submissiveness as a condition for attaining sexual gratification is a "perversion" that occurs fairly frequently in women and occasionally in men. Emphasis is displaced from one's own existence onto the personality of the partner. One lives only through

the partner, views oneself as nothing, the partner as everything, and is ready to make any sacrifice for the partner's
sake. "Falling in love" is perversion to the extent that sexual
excitement consists partially in the feeling of one's own
insignificance as compared with the magnificence of the
partner. This perversion may be a transitional state between
infatuation and masochism; the unconscious basis of the
perversion of extreme submissiveness is the fantasy of
belonging to the partner's body.

MASOCHISM AS PERVERSION

Masochism was originally observed and described in the
context of sexual perversion. Masochistic perversions may
be considered attenuated repetitions of childhood situations
and episodes wherein sexual fantasies, erotic games, strivings
towards sexual liaison with forbidden objects, especially the
mother, have encountered rejection in addition to real or
fantasied threat, punishment, or ridicule (Lowenstein,
1957). In perversion, the object who stands for the parent
joins into sexual play instead of disapproving. Thus threat
and punishment are modified. This is what lies at the core
of the masochistic perversion. By urging the sexual partner
to participate in a scene of castration threat or punishment,
the masochist forces the threatening, disapproving parent of
his childhood to undo his early rebuff. This repetition constitutes a veiled, incestuous gratification: "The masochistic
scene is thus a means of gratifying the forbidden, repressed,
incestuous fantasies but with the castration threat undone"
(Lowenstein, 1957).

According to Bieber (1966), masochism "integrates
with sexual activity as a defensive mechanism, to localize
and to circumscribe the extent of threat." Sexual patterns
as well as an interpersonal power system involving submis-

sion–domination are combined in masochistic sexuality. Punishment is tolerated by the masochist in expectation of injury for the sexual act. The sexual masochist usually prefers a specific and unique erotic stimulus: He may require a beating or prefer to be assaulted by a woman's leather heel, neither of which are interchangeable. Though there is a general notion that for the sexual masochist, pain accompanies sexual excitement, evidence does not bear this out. The threshold for awareness of pain is markedly increased in presence of rage and sexual excitation. Should pain be experienced during sexual activity, the excitation would, therefore, undoubtedly cease. Pain is not so much sought after as endured as a concomitant of, or stimulus to, the masochistic perversion. It is experienced after completion of the sexual act.

Though Freud and Krafft-Ebing postulate a physiological explanation for the tendency of painful stimuli to initiate or enhance sexual excitation, Bieber indicates that anxiety may similarly catalyze and sustain sexual excitation.

MASOCHISM AND BEATING FANTASIES

Bonaparte (1953) indicates beating fantasies are "typical" reactions of the normal girl to the oedipal conflict.

Rubinfine (1965) suggests beating fantasies are universal and are indications of a particular developmental phase just as are rescue fantasies. He feels they persist in patients where obsessive mechanisms prove incapable of guaranteeing the safety of their objects; beating fantasies are a means of protecting "good" objects as well as themselves against their sadistic impulses.

Beating fantasies and dreams of beating derive not so much from the anal–sadistic period as from the phallic period, proposes Schuster (1966). Primal scene experiences lead to sadomasochistic concepts of intercourse and to shifting identifications with both violent father and violated mother.

Lewis (1971) sees beating fantasies as "superego products." Within this framework, they appear as self-loving fantasies concomitant to self-hating ones, both yielding relief from shame. Since shame, according to Lewis, devolves on established identifications with an ego-ideal, beating fantasies need not point to instinctual regression. The vicarious pleasure experiences are products of one's longing to be loved and admired, enacted in fantasies about the self in the eyes of the "other." This offers an alternative explanation to Freud's notion that beating fantasies lead to sexual excitement: Sexual arousal is evoked, here, as a result of "triumph feelings" accompanying shame. The sexual arousal is equivalent to the triumph feeling, while the beating fantasies are the "cognitive" aspect of the humiliation feeling. Lewis suggests that "the self which is in both places experiences both in beating fantasies but with the humiliation feeling more distant." In addition, the "agreeableness" of the notion that "a child is being beaten" stems from the idea that humiliation is agreeable to the parent and thus to the child in identification with the punitive, parental image and his "righteous indignation."

THE MASOCHISTIC CHARACTER

Reich (1933) challenged Freud's emphasis on the inevitability of human suffering, and felt that Freud overlooked the importance of the frustrating, punishing outer world. His description of the "masochistic character" indicates that, subjectively, there is a pervasive sensation of suffering, externalized in complaints, chronic attitudes involving self-damage and self-depreciation, and a drive to torture others.

Masochistic characters also show a specifically awkward, "atactic" behavior in their relationships with others, not unlike some aspects of mental deficiency. Underlying their provocations lies an intense disillusionment in relation to those who insufficiently gratified them. Since the provocations are directed against those who are loved and from whom love is demanded, guilt feelings, as well as the fear of losing love, are increased.

Embodied in masochism is a combination of skin eroticism, anality, and fear of being left alone that the masochist tries to resolve by bodily contact: "Beat me" (or "warm me," "protect me") is a disguised expression of the excessive demand for love. The complex varieties of masochistic formation express an exaggerated, unfulfillable need for love, in addition to an unusual proneness for anxiety as starting point for the consequent rage that ensues when the demand is not met. Repression of the exhibitionistic impulses of the genital phase, as well as subsequent inhibition of further genital development, is specific regarding the masochistic character.

Thus masochistic characters cannot stand praise. Despite his high aspirations, one of Reich's patients could not tolerate being head of his class: "If I remained a good student I would feel as if I was standing in front of a crowd showing my erect penis."

Reich also proposed that masochism involved choice of a "lesser injury." He described a three-year-old child punished by his father for soiling:

The boy . . . turned on his stomach and waited for the beating with great curiosity mixed with anxiety. The blows were heavy but the boy had a feeling of relief. They were harmless compared to the anticipated injury to the genitals, and thus relieved him of a good deal of anxiety.

Reik (1941) perceives the masochistic character as a composite expression of aggressive, ambitious, revengeful, defiant impulses revealed in fantasy or circuitously in action and directed against an actual person or persons, though often with what is termed a "reversed sign." He emphasizes the importance of the sadistic fantasy, citing it as the "soil in which masochism grows." Far from feeling, as Reich did, that in masochism we see an "inhibited exhibitionism," he maintains that the "demonstrative" quality in parading one's harmlessness, generosity, ineptness, or suffering is, indeed, actual exhibitionism, with the aim of concealing something else: "hostile, stubborn, vain-glorious tyranny." "Victory through defeat" is his summation of this construct.

The reversal of all pleasure values usually considered indigenous to masochism is illusory, continues Reik. Actually, the masochist aims at the "same pleasure we all do," though in an indirect fashion. Intimidated by threatening anxiety, inhibited by the notion of punishment, beset by unconscious guilt feelings, he avoids anxiety and pursues pleasure by submitting to punishment, suffering, and humiliation voluntarily, triumphantly gaining the "right to enjoy the gratification denied before." The masochist does not accept punishment and humiliation but rather anticipates them, not only demonstrating the ineffectualness of the punitive forces in withholding the forbidden gratification but affirming that these forces actively assist him. By taking the role of the authority and chastising himself, he suspends punishment. By depreciating and disgracing himself, he transforms punishment into an "enticement." By clinging to discomfort, by insisting on pain and abasement, he spitefully shows that all inhibitive forces of education and culture must fail, since he, though pretending to submission, does not acquiesce in spirit. The masochist seeks to convey the meaninglessness of all attempts to have him give up gratification, by rendering punishment the condition of gratification. Masochism is thus characterized (Reik, 1941) by unconscious defiance in defeat, by the "secret foretaste and foreknowledge of coming conquest."

According to Fenichel (1945), masochistic characters enjoy exhibiting their misery: "Look how miserable I am" typically stands for "Look how miserable you made me." This masochistic behavior has accusing, blackmailing overtones. The sadism that has been turned against the ego in masochism is evidenced in the attempts made to force objects to give love or affection.

Skin eroticism, the erogenous basis of the fantasy of being beaten, is found in the longing for the warming proximity of the object, which, if not forthcoming, is obtained by self-torture. The typical conflict concerning persons with receptive longings—that between a sadistic destruction of the frustrating object and a masochistic total yielding to the object in the hope he will then not remain forever unavailable—is manifested in the syndrome "total submission, used for sadistic purposes."

MORAL MASOCHISM

The enjoyment of humiliation indicates that the idea of being father's sexual object, initially experienced as being beaten by father, has been further transformed into the idea of being beaten by God or destiny (Fenichel, 1945). Extreme instances of moral masochism represent attempts of the ego to cope with a harsh superego and include such contradictory devices as rebellion and ingratiation. One's own suffering is regarded as a manifestation of the degree of ingratiation or of the amount one is prepared to endure to gain father's forgiveness. At the same time it is an expression of protest, of demonstrating in a hostile manner the terrible deeds father is capable of committing.

Fenichel (1945) refers to the childhood history of a moral masochist with an extremely "weak father and a fantastic, religious, inconsistent and strict mother," who would constantly arouse the child's sexual feelings by excessive cuddling and then whip him when he tried to demonstrate his feelings. Apparently the whipping proved an externalization of the sexual relationship with his mother: "This relationship fixed his behavior not only toward other external objects but also toward his own superego, which was modeled after his mother." Receiving punishment from love objects seemed the only human exchange he could muster. However (Fenichel, 1945),

> a superficial obsequiousness actually concealed a profound rebellion against the standards of the model he had chosen. The unconscious passive desire to be beaten had been remodeled into a desire to be condemned, and the defensive fear of being beaten transformed into social anxiety.

Moral masochism and hypocrisy are similar inasmuch as morality is employed in both for purposes of gratification of deneutralized drives (Lowenstein, 1957). The masochistic gratification is unconscious in moral masochism, whereas the moral motivation may be conscious or not. In hypocrisy, the moral motivation is consciously stressed to conceal "preconscious gratifications of ego interests or of sadism." To some degree sadism of the superego is germane to hypocrisy. The difference therefore is that in sadism of the superego and in masochism of the ego the self is the victim, whereas in hypocrisy the gratification is elicited at the expense of others.

Guilt, both conscious and unconscious, concerning sexual and aggressive wishes towards the parent transforms sadism into masochism (Freud, 1905). Furthermore, the phenomenon of guilt assists in resolving the oedipal phase by creation of the superego, with its concomitant internalization of the multifaceted aspects of mother and father figures. In particular, identification with the threatening parent evokes "internalized threat" experienced as guilt. Identifications channeled by fear of parents may be followed by identifications involving admiration of them. Masochistic individuals remain unaware of the extent to which they fear and exaggerate moral failure.

Though there is no clear differentiation made between the terms conscience, need for punishment, and guilt, Freud (1923) stated that the tension between the demands of conscience and the actual attainments of the ego is subjectively experienced as a sense of guilt. Piers and Singer (1953) suggest that though the tension between ego and superego evokes guilt, that between ego-ideal and superego evokes feelings of shame. The sense of shame or failure to live up to one's ego-ideal is less explored than the sense of guilt based on castration threat. Shame and guilt are usually grouped together because of their common function as drive controls. Guilt is focused on as the generic term for both shame and guilt, to the neglect of specific shame phenomena. Shame has been regarded as a lower order of guilt or precursor of guilt in the development of moral values. Lewis (1971) suggests both shame and guilt are equally, though differently, advanced superego processes developed along different routes of identification. Identification with the threatening parent evokes internalized threat, experienced as guilt. Identification with the admired ego-ideal stimulates pride and triumphant feelings; failure to abide by the admired imago evokes shame. In guilt, the ideational or value system is the focal point. In shame, awareness of self with reference to the internalized "other" is crucial.

Lewis further points to contrasts in superego style in relation to whether ego-ideal or sense of guilt is invoked. Guilt-prone individuals function on the basis of internalized, punitive parental figures, seek to deflect the threatened punishment rather than deal with the self vis-à-vis others, direct "righteous indignation" against the self, and project aggression. Shame phenomena are more varied and differ from each other as, for example, the spectrum of humiliation, humiliated fury, mortification, embarrassment, chagrin, and shyness. Shame is more difficult for the adult to master than guilt inasmuch as functioning of the self is interfered with. This is shown in competitive defeat, sexual rebuff, feelings of being ridiculed by others, social slights, or invasion of privacy. Shame also involves loss of self-esteem, hostility directed against the self, tendency to a sense of failure. Shame and guilt produce different forms of symptom formation: Thus, the connection between shame and depression, between guilt, obsessive neurosis, and paranoia.

MASOCHISM AS A "NORMAL" PHENOMENON

There is considerable evidence that some moral masochistic impulses are essential if we are to "feel content with ourselves and are to make a satisfactory social adjustment" (De Monchy, 1950). There is a desire to feel useful or be needed by another, to serve a doctrine or social cause. For most, some degree of self-sacrifice and a need for effacement or subordination of self to a higher authority are deeply rooted longings. In infancy the emotional dependence of the child regarding parents reflects masochistic tendencies. Also pertinent later on is the individual's need to become part of a larger unit where one ceases, to some extent, to be independent or relinquishes one's personal existence as, for example, in one's attitude towards a leader.

The difference between the normal and masochistic character is one of degree rather than kind, in the view of Brenner (1959). Given the psychic equipment of the child—his instinctual drives and ego capacities on the one hand and his environment on the other, which includes available gratifications and inescapable frustrations—it seems unavoidable that some degree of suffering should reside in psychic functioning. Brenner suggests that masochistic formations are pervasive in both normal and neurotic individuals. Since a need for punishment concerning oedipal conflicts and fantasies, conscious or unconscious, is inevitably subsumed in the emergence of normal superego processes, some form of masochism is ubiquitous.

In all ages man has "denied and abused" himself, and this type of behavior has been greatly esteemed particularly when it has been ritualized in various religious practices (Salzman, 1959). Mortification, for example, has been considered a highly efficacious and moral activity auguring great rewards and frequently leading to sainthood. By emphasizing bodily injury or neglect, mortification negates mere bodily processes and exalts spiritual values. Similar to the mortifier, the masochist aspires to "some higher need by a process of active denial or self punishment." Masochistic behavior, despite its self-injuring implications, may be considered a wish for mastery and an "adjustive maneuver designed to deal with certain personal and social conditions." Masochism is a "universal technique employed by man through the ages to deal with such problems of existence as guilt, helplessness and powerlessness" (Salzman, 1959).

Actually any tendency latently pleasurable but culturally taboo could constitute the theme of the masochistic dynamism, which may explain the universality of masochistic formations since taboos on certain pleasurable activities have accompanied the human condition in all ages. Sex, which subsumes both pleasurable and tabooed components, is pointed out as relevant in this context.

MASOCHISM AND HUMOR

Dooley (1941) asserts that humor may emerge during analysis, concomitant to the patient's resignation in regard to the thwarting of oedipal wishes. The ego, via playful fantasy, seeks restoration of the parent's love by then claiming the love of the parent's successor, the superego. That is, to avoid further loss, the destructive drives are placed under the aegis of the superego, while the ego "plays" with them, thereby turning defeat into victory. This can be achieved, however, in the event aggression is renounced and a masochistic attitude appears. Subordination of the ego to the superego and an acceptance of pain are decisive. Reduction of the pain may occur by envisaging the ego or drives denuded of their power, as though they were small children. The reduced ego is thus freed of responsibility and guilt, and the adult superego appears "amused" at the irresponsibility of the ego.

In this mechanism of humor, two parts of the personality, actor and observer, seem to participate. The ego is split into two,[1] suffering child and liberated child, as though "living in two persons."

---

[1] Wittels (1937) also describes a similarly split ego in masochism, postulating one part that "saves itself" by imposing all suffering on the other part, thus seeking to annihilate the latter.

Brenman (1952) in describing one of her patients as a "comic teasee" or "sly jester," suggests that denial and reaction formation are counterposed to need and hate. Here generosity and self-sacrifice disguise hostile, engulfing lavishness. Aggression is both expressed and held within limits by the teasee's witty unmasking of others, while seemingly caricaturing herself. Brenman's patient is described as "desperately ingratiating and oversolicitous" from a very early age in response to her mother; the mother contemptuously designated these actions "fawning." As the patient's role in the family as "teasee" was reinforced, she continued to be increasingly ridiculed and scapegoated by her mother. In addition to her patient's self-abnegating and engulfingly "giving" attitudes, Brenman pointed to the characteristic projective mechanisms in her preferred modes of defense. She all too readily felt "let down," misled, picked-on, and betrayed by setting up situations inevitably estranging those she cared for.

When the ego can no longer retain this balance, that is, when threatened by loss of love, there is an impoverishment of the defensive and adaptive–creative ego functions. A diminution of the controls usually provided by the defenses and the synthesizing functions of the ego sets in, so that infantile need and rage emerge. Teasing presumably lies between aggression and love. Should one relinquish this middle position, one's behavior may emerge as pointed wit, or when clearly hostile, as ridicule, mockery, or derision. Alternately when it is socially adaptive, it becomes humorous banter. Also, the middle position of teasee may give way to a continuum of behaviors ranging from masochistic provocation of an actual attack to the sublimation of a comic performance, where the individual becomes the one laughed at yet maintains control by deliberately offering entertainment at his own expense.

Fromm (1941) finds that in Western society, masochistic and sadistic strivings assist the individual in escaping unbearable feelings of aloneness and powerlessness. Man seeks for something or someone to tie himself to and tries frantically to eliminate the self and its "burden" of freedom. Consequently, in some situations, these masochistic strivings are relatively successful, as in submission to a leader under fascism. The sadomasochistic character admires authority and tends to submit, yet desires the ascendant role as well, so that others may defer to him. In response to irrational authority, resentment and opposition inevitably arise; leading to conflict and suffering, with no possibility of resolution. As such these feelings are repressed, replaced by blind admiration that eliminates the painful and dangerous implications of one's rebelliousness.

Kardiner (1945) views the personality structure of Western man as attuned to the requirements of the feudal system. The aggressions concomitant to discipline are checked by a system of rewards for obedience after death. When this reward system lost vogue, the basic personality structure was not correspondingly changed. Aggression turned either into channels of self-abnegation, as in Puritanism, or into competition for the new opportunities for self-validation. The anxieties of Western man are, according to this author, concerned with success as a form of self-realization, as salvation was in the Middle Ages. For modern man, failure brings with it not so much social censure as it does self-hatred, feelings of inferiority, and hopelessness.

Examining the growth cycle for factors that create anxiety, Kardiner indicates that initially there is a strong foundation for optimal personality growth. Disciplinary factors that inflict most damage pertain to the sexual taboos.

These punitive measures introduce a "pain element" that facilitates guilt, as well as obedience patterns that are incompatible with social goals. Hence, they become the focus of conflicts, destroy self-esteem, and foster self-contempt and hatred of the parent. Frustrations regarding these sexual disciplines, according to Kardiner, create neurosis, psychosomatic disorders, masochistic syndromes, and degradation of the sexual impulse of man where the "female is the chief victim."

MASOCHISM AS DEFENSE

Berliner, in a series of penetrating papers (1940, 1942, 1947, 1958), appears as the first thinker to interject fresh concepts within the Freudian framework insofar as his linking of masochistic phenomena with early parent–child interactions is concerned. He feels that the so-called sexual masochist is at the same time a moral masochist, i.e., the perversion is concomitant to a character formation that the pervert and moral masochist share. He promulgates the view that masochism is neither an instinctual force nor the person's sadism turned around upon the self but rather points to a "disturbance of object relations," a "pathological way of loving." Superego and transference manifestations take the place of the original, sadistic love object. Furthermore, masochism is the search for love or, in sexual perversion, for sexual pleasure, through the troubled context of displeasure originally "forced upon the subject." Thereafter, the search for gratification of erotic needs is oriented in a specifically masochistic direction. Masochism is the "neurotic solution of an infantile conflict between the need for being loved on the level of oral and skin erotism, and the actual experience of non-love coming from the person whose love is needed." Also, masochism emerges as a "defensive structure" counterposed to the experience of "non-love."

Similar in her frame of reference, Menaker (1953) concurs with Berliner's view of masochism as inherently a function of the ego, "for purposes of maintaining a vitally needed love relationship to a primary object." However, she feels the loss of identity and feelings of worthlessness indigenous to the moral masochist lie in far more primitive levels of ego development than Berliner describes. Menaker proffers as her hypothesis that masochism

> originates at the oral level of infantile development, that it is the outcome of traumatic deprivation, that it functions as a defense against experiencing this deprivation with its concomitant anxiety and aggression, and that it is a means of perpetuating whatever bond there is to the mother.

The masochistic response, according to Bieber (1966), constitutes a typical defense against anticipation of injury for self-enhancing behavior, though this behavior may actually be personally and socially syntonic. Masochistic defenses are especially noted in competitive spheres, that is, in the fear of provoking antagonism regarding one's successful performance. This defensive adaptation to threat may be evidenced in patients with severe work inhibitions, who aim to avoid retaliation from feared competitors.

MASOCHISM AND SYMPTOM FORMATION

Both sexual and aggressive instincts are central in the formation of symptoms (Gero, 1962). The aggressive instinct operates in those aspects of symptom formation connected with the superego, while the sexual instinct prevails in symptom formations where the primary process, and repression as withdrawal of cathexis, contribute to the pathologic process. Gero points to a distinction between aggressive and sadomasochistic drives, especially in considering sadism and masochism as component instincts of the sexual drive, in consonance with Freud's original theory. Since the sexual and aggressive drives participate in separate aspects of symptom formation, one's elucidation of a clinical problem or symptom, in addition to one's therapeutic interpretations of them, seem affected by differing conceptions of sadomasochism and aggression.

In differentiating sadomasochistic from aggressive drives, Gero suggests one can trace the derivatives of the sexual drive if one can prove that the fantasy or action in question was originally connected with sexual excitement. Aggressive fantasies come readily to consciousness, whereas sadistic fantasies remain repressed. Of all the variegated processes of the sexual drive, the sadomasochistic drive patterns of the phallic phase have an especially important role in the formation of symptoms.

PSYCHIC MASOCHISM

Bergler (1949) has written extensively on what he terms "psychic masochism" manifested in the so-called "triad of oral mechanisms." Through their behavior, or by distortion of external situations, neurotics unconsciously provoke disappointment, refusal, or humiliation, identifying the outer world with the refusing, preoedipal mother. Repressing their initial provocation, they become pseudoaggressive, behaving with righteous indignation and seemingly in self defense. After experiencing the rebuff and retaliativeness that they unconsciously seek, they feel victimized and self-pitying.

Bergler's orientation is of interest, and his work is vast in clinical documentation, though there is a mechanical inevitability to his theory that "psychic masochism" is the result of early oral disappointments or narcissistic wounds to "autarchic omnipotence." According to his theory, should mother delay with breast or bottle, a collapse of "childhood megalomania" ensues. Bergler suggests this construct as an extension of the work of Melanie Klein who, he felt, neglected masochistic components in behavior.

The masochistic defense has its origins in the sense of disappointment of absolute love from the mother (Millet, 1959). The masochist's image of himself as a worthy object, with freedom to progress to more differentiated areas of pleasure has its essential basis in the self-image that he derives from the "introjection of his mirror-image which he fantasies reflected from the mirror of his mother's love." Should the individual not perceive this image clearly, or if it changes form too frequently, he may be

> destined to stay rooted to this spot . . . and continue . . . to struggle for some release from this predicament of doubt; as to his essential worth, his motives, the intentions of others towards him, as to whether he can ever be relieved of these torturing doubts.

The struggle may end in psychosis, suicidal episodes, acceptance of a life of self-denial in martyrdom, or in religious asceticism.

NARCISSISTIC MORTIFICATION

By imagining or producing scenes of torture or punishment that he himself creates, the masochist avoids being tortured or punished in an unexpected and uncontrollable way. Eidelberg (1959) perceives the masochistic aim as "narcissistic mortification," expressing a sense of unfair punishment and humiliation. The aggressive wishes and exhibitionism of the masochist are warded off by identifying with the sadist who both punishes and humiliates him. Perhaps in provoking humiliating defeat from a parent or parent substitute, the masochist retains his infantile omnipotence, fostering the illusion he can control his parent. To the masochist, his "ability" to produce failure and provoke punishment serves as proof of his magical control of the environment, restores his infantile feeling of omnipotence, and avoids the narcissistic mortification accompanying helplessness.

Bychowsky (1959) finds Eidelberg's concept of "narcissistic mortification" useful but seeks to elaborate it further. Discharge of aggression and repression of narcissistic libido are engendered by narcissistic mortification as prerequisite for the formation of what is termed the "masochistic bond." Quanta of aggressive "energy" are directed at the original object, with the aim of destroying the object or emphasizing his defeat. In consonance with mourning processes, the original object is not abandoned but incorporated within the self: "Narcissistic libido dammed up by the shock of mortification serves to recathect the self and internalized parental image, now endowed with increasing power." Thus, the masochistic bond is established, with emphasis falling more and more on the presumably strong and powerful parent whose affection and care "can be purchased only at the price of primitive weakness and abject surrender." In a process called "release of introjects," relationships in the present assume the same role as the original objects.

MASOCHISM AND INCORPORATION

Blumstein's (1959) clinical experiences led him to the belief that masochism is associated with fantasies and acts of self-preparation for being incorporated. The fantasied and actual self-destruction has as its unconscious aim the goal of achieving a secure and physically gratifying union with an omnipotent figure.

MASOCHISM AND NARCISSISM

In discussing the "Role of Narcissism in Moral Masochism" Bernstein (1957) states that the child's primary narcissism gradually evolves into object love and contributes to the formation of an ego-ideal. Narcissism is relinquished when there has been optimal rapport with parents in consonance with the child's needs. Should the parents themselves prove narcissistic and depriving, the child regresses to his own "narcissistic satisfactions." Describing three of his patients, Bernstein indicates they felt "instruments of their parents' narcissistic needs" from earliest childhood, leading to distorted development of the ego, exaggeratedly dependent parental attachments and marked oral fixations and regression. The child's body attributes, ego functions, and instinctual drives seemed in the service of the parental narcissism and immature instinctual drives. Masochistic behavior serves as protection against the danger of object loss.

Should actual or threatened loss occur, introjection of the object ensues with merging of self-image and ambivalent object. Oedipal disappointment is experienced as both a narcissistic and oral trauma with accompanying feelings of loss, helplessness, and rage. It is dealt with in the same manner as the pregenital trauma of separation or loss by introjection of the object and regressive splitting of object and self-representations with defusion of libidinal and aggressive feelings. The superego becomes the "sadistic idealized parent-child," while the ego becomes the "hated, devalued parent-child." In this "endopsychic manner the child–parent relationship is regressively restored." Masochistic relationships in adult life are repetitive reenactments of childhood experiences and fantasies in which the patient has the illusion he actively controls the situation formerly passively endured.

Kohut (1966) proposes that the preconscious correlates of the narcissistic self and ego-ideal may be experienced as our ambitions and ideals. Ideals are capable of absorbing a considerable degree of transformed narcissistic libido and thus of diminishing narcissistic tension and vulnerability. Should the ego's "instinctual investment of the superego remain insufficiently desexualized," moral masochism follows; in short the ego feels humiliated in failing to live up to its ideals.

In the event our ambitions are unrealized and narcissistic–exhibitionistic tensions remain undischarged, the ego experiences disappointment and shame. Should traumatic onslaughts on the child's self-esteem drive the grandiose fantasies of the narcissistic self into repression, the adult ego then vacillates between an irrational overestimation of the self and feelings of inferiority and will react with narcissistic mortification to the thwarting of ambitions.

MASOCHISM AND CRIMINALITY

Freud described "criminals out of guilt feeling" who commit criminal acts because unconscious guilt feelings trouble them so severely that they hope some kind of punishment may bring relief (1915a).

Both masochist and psychopath feel "powerless and worthless, cheated and abused" and hope to obtain justice for their demands, claims Salzman (1960). They employ exploitative means for achieving their goals, the masochist relying upon his weakness, the psychopath upon the grandiosity that distinguishes him from others.

In an evaluation of Aichhorn's active techniques, which encourage establishment of a narcissistic transference in the treatment of juvenile delinquents, Kohut (1971) suggests that these are "emergency measures" necessary for optimal rapport with the analyst. They create a "transference-like focusing of the grandiose self and/or of the idealized parent imago upon him," preventing the patient from terminating therapy in the initial phase. One must ask, however, whether the actively created transference pertains to a delinquent, grandiose self or to the overestimated parent image. The inclination to form an emotional bond with the analyst suggests that an idealized parent image and the longing to form an idealizing transference were preconsciously present, though denied and concealed. There is, in addition, an:

> unconscious fear of a traumatic rejection of their idealizing attitude by the idealized object, or the anticipation of a traumatic disillusionment with the idealized object—a dread . . . of frustrations in the narcissistic realm which would lead to intolerable narcissistic tensions and to the painful experience of shame and hypochondria.

SEDUCTION OF THE AGGRESSOR

According to Lowenstein (1957) the mechanism of "seduction of the aggressor," ostensibly present in all children, manifests ingredients of future masochistic behavior. He refers to a predilection for situations involving danger, fear, and unpleasantness, as well as the concomitant attenuation, by way of the "loving, erotic complicity of the threatening parent." Pleasure in this behavior is found not in pain but in its removal, in cessation of the threat, thus involving a loving reunion with the parent. Eventually the induction of unpleasure and its removal are joined: Thus, there is considerable enjoyment of danger and threat via fairy tales, horror stories, and the like. Central to this sense of gratification is the reassurance that one is loved by the parent and that the threats are not real. The child plays at being naughty or at being punished with the forbidding or punishing adult, who in turn only plays at scolding and punishing him, soon relieving the child's distress by reassuringly loving behavior. Lowenstein describes this phenomenon as "protomasochism" or "premasochism," so long as genital involvement is absent. The protomasochistic role with the parent as aggressor is useful in preparing the child to deal with frustrations and danger. Also, in the author's view, it is the precursor of true masochistic phenomena.

INTERPERSONAL APPROACH

Sullivan (1945), in his enumeration of substitutive states, indicates that algolagnic people appear to enjoy suffering and, furthermore, communicating this to others. They have an astigmatic slant on life, such that its unpleasant aspects predominantly concern them. In addition, states Sullivan:

> a large number of people go to extraordinary lengths to get themselves imposed on, abused, humiliated . . . but as you go on, you discover this quite often pays, i.e., they get the things they want. And the things they want are satisfaction and security from anxiety.

Sullivan is discussing a pattern that allays anxiety and gives the illusion of security. Through suffering, the individual is excused from taking a positive part in life and usually manages to find someone to look after him.

In exploring the areas of interpersonal insecurity that might be resolved by suffering, Thompson (1959) points to passive dependency as an outstanding trait. Investigating the origin and dynamics of the masochistic pattern, she finds that in such cases there has been little or no affection from either parent. The parents, in constant battle, can however be seduced into a show of concern should the child demonstrate he has suffered. This is the closest approximation to "love" the child ever achieves. The child thus becomes adept in eliciting concern or guilt from the parents and thereby obtaining some degree of compensatory attention. Alternatively he succeeds in getting them to fight with one another, which puts him in the position of the innocent victim. This pattern of exaggerated assumption of blame or penchant for martyrdom then becomes a way of life.

INTEGRATIVE APPROACH

Waelder (1936) has pointed out that every psychic act may be viewed as a compromise among the various parts of the psychic apparatus. He employs the concept of multiple function in exploring the clinical phenomena of the masochistic character. In this light many of the presumably unrelated explanations having to do with unconscious motivation in masochistic behavior may be perceived as coexistent in the same patient and as mutually cooperative. Thus, a single set of masochistic fantasies and behaviors may serve an immense variety of functions.

Similar in her approach, Brenman (1952) suggests that the ambiguities permeating the literature on masochism arise from the fruitless attempts to channel a variety of highly organized, multifaceted clinical phenomena as function of one or another of the three psychic structures; id, ego, or superego. This has led some to consider masochism an instinct, partial instinct, defense mechanism, or superego formation. Brenman feels, however, that the complexities of masochistic formations cannot be attributed to any specific, structural concept.

A more sophisticated psychoanalytic theory, particularly pertaining to ego psychology, would enable us to break down into its components various psychological functions often regarded as simple, unitary expressions of one or another of the three psychic structures. The concept of the "motivational hierarchy," involving a many-leveled stratification of motivations functioning as mobile or bound cathexes, may emerge as the impetus for analysis of any complex psychological phenomenon: an isolated character trait; a chronic affect; a "lifestyle;" an alteration in a state of consciousness; or an illustration of the "comic teasee," a social role.

By way of illustration, Brenman discusses the role of "comic teasee" as one possible emergent in a masochistic character. This role is seen as a characterological expression of a masochistic development, that is, as a complex configuration specifically designed not only to encompass an unconscious need for punishment but also to maintain a balance between primitive libidinal and aggressive drives and four specific mechanisms of defense: introjection, denial, reaction formation, and projection. In addition, specific ego-adaptive functions play a decisive role. One or another of these components may come to the fore clinically, depending on the existing efficiency of ego functioning at the time. Brenman particularly emphasizes the central role of projective mechanisms in masochistic formations, especially the need to defend oneself against hostile impulses: The masochist assumes that others are as deprived as he, and he must therefore be constantly "giving." When his adaptation is optimal, he presents his objects with the emotional supplies he hopes to receive from them. As the aggressive aspect in his ambivalence emerges, his "giving" appears as a hostile, smothering endeavor to control, frequently felt by the object not as a gift but an enslavement. There is, in addition, a projection of aggressive impulses as well as a testing approach to all interactions with others, with the conviction that his difficulties and frustrations are due to the other. Apparently "he is ready to feel exploited as a direct consequence of his projected exploitativeness" (Brenman, 1952).

Eisenbud (1967) claims that the mechanisms involved in masochism emerge when there are no "alternative structures" available, that is, when the child's attempt at mastery or control has culminated in utter defeat in relation to "a personal opposing force." The child then seeks to repeat the situation, more to undo the failure than to gain the satisfaction previously desired. According to the author, loss of "efficacy" may disrupt the ego's motivational hierarchy, so that adaptive behavior results in a continuum of bizarre, fixated, perhaps masochistic, efforts to restore the loss.

Many of these papers emerge as brilliant additions to theory. They serve as variations, extensions, and elaborations of Krafft-Ebing's and Freud's basic themes. Some are more culturally oriented; others are steeped in Freud's biological or instinctual framework. Clearly pertinent to the point of view crystallized in this book are the formulations presented by Berliner and Menaker. Their contribution briefly lies in the following: emphasis on object relations, with particular stress on preoedipal experiences; view of masochism as a defense rather than as predominantly based in instinctual processes, i.e., as defense against awareness of the early oral deprivation and therefore, as a means of avoiding separation; perception that it is not one's own sadism but rather the sadism of the love object that is turned against the self; and the debunking of the accretion of thinking concerning the inherent guilt of the child for instinctual aggressions, placing responsibility on parents whose ambivalent attitudes initially set up the sadomasochistic interactions. Brenman's concept of "motivational hierarchy" points to a many-leveled stratification of motivations as a starting point for analyzing any complex psychological phenomenon. In this frame of reference, she views masochistic formations as reflecting infantile need and rage "pitted against" a variety of intermediary defense mechanisms, in interaction with available adaptive ego functions. Her approach is an eminently laudable attempt to reconcile the disparate points of view pervading the literature on masochism.

IV. Clinical Illustrations

The following are intensive clinical reports based on a perusal of therapy sessions as well as projective test responses of individuals who have been in analysis with me and whose life experiences illustrate various nuances of masochistic behavior. The clinical data, in its recurrent themes, will enable us to formulate the developmental trends or integrating techniques inherent in masochistic personalities. Inasmuch as masochistic features are found in all psychic functioning and personality is multifaceted, it does not seem feasible to complicate the existing diagnostic categories by isolating a construct such as "masochistic personality" or "masochistic character." When masochistic formations are central in the psychodynamic defense process, as well as in characterological or developmental configurations in the individual, however, one may speak in terms of a predominance of masochistic trends.

PATIENT B.

B., age 27, sought analysis because of her tremendous ambivalence regarding men; her inability to work through her unresolved rage and sexual involvement with her previous, male therapist; her frustrated need for nurturance concerning mother figures; her feelings of inadequacy regarding her unfulfilling work situation; and her lifelong sense of self-depreciation and freakishness.

B. hails from a nouveau riche New England family of mixed religious background. Her father, despite his lack of schooling, rose from a nondescript factory job to an important executive position in an industrial organization. Though the father was the nurturing, maternal, primal parent during her childhood, he later proved a decidedly sadistic and punitive, as well as seductive and invasive figure, the undisputed authority at home. He was the parent B. clearly preferred as a child. Except in transferential fantasies, dreams, and displacements regarding other men, the patient had largely repressed her resentment and rage regarding her father's arbitrary attitudes toward her. As she grew up, she "despised" his materialistic values.

B. contracted asthma as a young child.[1] She was deci-

_____

[1] The nuclear psychodynamic conflict in asthma centers on an excessive, unresolved dependency regarding the mother figure. Hostile impulses that threaten the dependency situation, as well as any sudden effort that may call for independent functioning, may revive the deep-seated conflict between independent and dependent tendencies

dedly not fond of being held by her mother. "I always preferred being held by my father. If my mother sang, I would cry. If father held me, it would soothe me." Her mother, though better educated than her father, appeared to be a fairly undeveloped, parasitical, conforming, puritanical, mother-attached individual, who managed to elicit a barrage of critical behavior from her husband. The parents were estranged from, and distant with, one another. The patient insists that even at an early age she found her mother "boring" and uninteresting. She felt completely alienated from her mother's narrow, conventional values and appeared more clearly identified with male activities. B. always felt the mother preferred her younger sister, born when patient was three. Her sister had been more acceptably feminine, though B. displayed greater adeptness in intellectual areas.

The home seemed antiseptic and cold: "My house was like a tomb." The patient was forbidden to invite friends of another nationality or of a lower socioeconomic group; nor could she bring anyone above the first floor. Her mother, who listened to the patient's conversations on the telephone, was considered invasive and untrustworthy. According to the mother, B. was regularly "bad" or naughty; her actions were duly reported to the father, who beat her with a yardstick. There appeared to be a constant battle between the patient and her mother: "I looked down upon mother, talked back, was contemptuous, and she knew it. She always made me feel guilty. She would trick me. Since they made me feel guilty, I felt as though I deserved punishment."

---

and precipitate an attack. A combination of unconscious parental seduction and overt rejection is another common finding in the history of asthma cases as is birth of a sibling who threatens to absorb mother's attention. Whenever B. had an attack, her mother would be more solicitous.

She acknowledges "secret satisfaction when father would beat mother down. Wanted him to be the authority he was." Her mother, in B.'s associations, emerged as a disturbed, malevolent, unaffirmative, as well as ineffectual, contact-depriving figure, desiring to pull B. into her orbit of suffering and unhappiness. Yet there is the undeniable suggestion that the father's early seduction of the patient and authoritarian disregard for her mother, facilitated the mother's anxieties and rejection of the patient. Leaving the church, a repudiation of their mutual interest in religion, proved B.'s final rejection of her mother. When her mother died, B. showed little affect. She recalls that on one occasion, shortly before her death, the mother, ravaged by illness, asked B. for help or support in going upstairs to her room; B. refused.

B. was defiant, a decided tomboy. She recalls masturbatory fantasies concerning two men in combat that disturbed her a good deal; she alternately identified with both victor and victim.[1] On discovering B. masturbating, her parents were severely punitive, a highly traumatic experience for B. During her adolescence they discouraged boy friends and dating quite thoroughly. Mother would criticize the way B. acted, talked, walked, or dressed. Father would demand a bearhug when he got home, which she resented; he would repulse her should she make an overture to him. Or he would squeeze her so hard it would hurt. When she fussed, he said, "I will, if I want." B. frequently stated the sole relationship with her parents was "being a bad girl."

B. felt she was grotesque and masculine and appeared convinced she was homosexual. A distorted head appeared

---

[1] Lowenstein (1957) describes beating fantasies in a patient who identified consciously with the powerful, cruel, sadistic figures in the imagined scenes; unconsciously, however, the patient identified with a slave denied sexual gratification and aroused by the denial.

in one of her dreams: "an inhuman, grotesque thing . . . afraid of peeling off the layers." In college, however, a close relationship with a girl friend affirmed her humanness. Despite B.'s self-criticism, she is, in actuality, an extremely attractive and well-groomed female.

After college, where she was considered a gifted student, B. left home and worked for several years in unrewarding, clerical jobs where she felt unappreciated, unfulfilled, and highly resentful of authority figures, whose jobs she envied and felt she could handle better. She could not resolve the conflicts regarding her work-orientation until fairly recently. Though often catapulted into despair because of her hypersensitivity over some interpersonal deficiency, she now has a more responsible and stimulating position where she feels more productive and socially useful.

B. has related to her sister as though the sister, not she, were the older or parenting one. During the period she and her sister shared an apartment, B. seemed utterly dependent on her, frequently permitted her to seduce B.'s own boy friends. Occasionally her pathological jealousy and rage regarding the sister would erupt.

Relationships with men have been severely disturbed. On a date, she is guarded, distorting the culturally based arrangements as an assertion of male superiority designed to humiliate her, probably an outgrowth of her perception of her father's rigidly authoritarian role in the family. Once she embarks on a heterosexual relationship, her bristling suspiciousness permeates the entire situation, though it is masked by deferential acquiescence.

B. tends to feel victimized or used, considers men powerful and manipulative and sex an assault or attack. At the same time she is generally obeisant, clingingly dependent, or passively rejecting. There is sometimes an overexaltation of men: They appear as foreign, exotic creatures. Recently, she described a bright young man she was dating, who had varied, somewhat dilettantish interests, as a "genius, a Leonardo da Vinci." With him, as with others, she all too swiftly engaged in sexual practices over which she later felt humiliated and ashamed. When the relationship is over there is a long, bleak period of attrition; B. is then seeped in retaliatory and vengeful fantasies.

B.'s self-conception is derived from an identification with her parents' criticism, rejection, invasiveness, and engulfment. There is some degree of identification with the victimized role, obtained from her mother, who felt exploited and domineered by father, in addition to a distorted, self-propelled continuation of her own earlier experience of father as both sadistic and eroticizing, which she interjects into heterosexual situations. She has had fantasies concerning sexual intercourse where "the man urinates on the woman,"[1] or "is in her front and back;" these are humiliating and debasing experiences. She can become aroused only when she visualizes such a fantasy, i.e., the male as ogre, and herself in a degraded or masochistic role. She communicated a dream that involved "being sat on . . . I can't get out from under," similar to the feeling emanating from all men, with father as prototype. "If someone loves me, I feel terrible—it's like a trap I can't get out of." Father, she felt, would buy her affection.

Currently, B. is seeking to divest men of their godlike and forbidding attitudes and has begun to comprehend her own role in provoking rejection. Significantly, she has now begun to acknowledge and express anger and rage regard-

---

[1] Freud (1908) describes the child who "cannot guess that out of the male organ another substance can be expelled besides urine" and the "innocent" girl on her wedding night who is still indignant because the man has "urinated into her."

ing her father or authority figures in an emotional rather than intellectual mode.

Towards me, her attitudes have been overidealizing, as is her wont with many female authority figures. Her expectations were that I would be mechanical or authoritarian as was father. Her homosexual predilections have been in the direction of an adolescent-like crush or a desire for tactile closeness; for example, in one of her dreams concerning the analyst, she sat on the floor leaning against me, her head on my knee: "You put your hand on my head." Where hostility occurred towards me, it was covert or provocative, rarely direct, or was manifested in her demanding dependency. Our relationship was a friendly one; I sought to eliminate as much as possible the trappings of the analytic format, though not more than proved comfortable for me. B. often called me at my home if she was in a panic, which was not infrequent. I encouraged her to consult with me if she required information or collaboration where her exploration of various feminine activities, hitherto avoided, were concerned, i.e., in furnishing her apartment, and so on.

PATIENT C.

C., 28, youngest of three children born to Jewish, foreign-born, lower-middle-class parents, initiated therapy on the suggestion of his physician because of gastrointestinal symptoms.

C. was decidedly unwanted. He was told by his mother he was a repulsive looking infant covered with skin eruptions and considered a "bag of garbage." So compliant was he that toilet training was completed by the time he reached his first birthday. His earliest memory has to do with his reluctance to attend school. His mother, overwhelmed by unconscious guilt for her early lack of maternal concern, infantilized and overprotected C., designating this as affection, while preventing him from developing an autonomous ego.

The patient remembers his mother as constantly verbalizing her suffering, mostly in connection with the shortcomings of his father and the burdens of motherhood. Also, she was herself overly attached to and attendant on her own mother, who lived in the apartment above. Completely dissociated by the patient was the mother's complaining, nagging, martyred role and the fact that his father, despite her protestations, was a steady provider.

C.'s father attended the equivalent of college in Europe, resumed his studies here, but eventually succumbed to the essentially unsatisfying, exhaustive demands of his job as a clerk, where he worked excessively long hours and derived an ineffectual income. He is considered a failure by his wife. As a child, C. considered his father as silent, brutish, tremendously powerful, and physically capable, though markedly dependent on his wife for emotional succor. The relationship between father and patient was meager, almost nonexistent. Once C. accepted the blame for some naughtiness of his sister's, for which his father administered a beating. C. did this, he claims, to obtain father's attention. He feels a failure just as father does. Father could have seized the opportunity to get out of the "crumby existence" their family lives in, but he proved fearful of making any change. "I'm like that too," exclaims C.

Two vivid childhood experiences emerge. When C. was examined by the doctor for undescended testicles, he felt tremendously humiliated by his mother's presence and subsequent comments, and he has been haunted by a fear of abnormality regarding his genitals. The other experience occurred during a summer vacation when he and his parents shared one room. C. overheard them having intercourse and felt his father was cruel and sadistic. He was certain his father forced himself on his mother, another indication of her suffering. He grew up with the conviction that sex was painful to women and was, in sum, an animalistic affair.

As a child, C. was regularly obedient, conforming, and markedly dependent on mother. He was frequently mother's companion, proved a willing recipient of all her complaints, and sided completely with her in parental squabbles. Later, he would assume the role of family chauffeur, driving his father's car, with his mother seated in front next to him and his father in back! This manipulation seemed guaranteed to elicit father's rage and reinforced as well his identification with an undermined and cast-off parent.

His older siblings were married at the time the patient started therapy. Previously, C.'s older brother was the mother's confidante. It almost seemed C. circumscribed his life in order to gather the few crumbs cast by mother, whom he now could have all to himself.

During childhood there were few or no friends. C. would return home immediately on completing school for fear of discommoding mother. He had never been away from home and would fear getting lost, even when grown up. C. has lived in a marginal neighborhood, in the same apartment, all his life.

After attending college for one year, he literally fled in the throes of a delayed adolescent or sexual crisis. There was also some fear of superseding his father. He appeared immobilized by the "outside world" and could not cope with the social implications of encountering girls in his class for the first time. Some indications of homosexual panic seemed evident in his reluctance to be exposed in the gym period or while taking showers. He felt, despite his large frame and rather attractive appearance, that his body was ugly and effeminate and was convinced he had female-like breasts and plump hips. During masturbatory fantasies, he would sometimes beat himself on the buttocks or fantasize he was in the female role.[1]

The patient possesses considerable technical skill and works in the same field as his brother. He never obtained a degree, however, which would involve him in more challenging areas. Aside from work, for the most part, he has circumscribed his life, remained at home, watched TV, or accompanied his parents in visits to relatives. The notion of leaving home, even for a brief vacation, was terrifying. Once, as a young man, C. dated a girl for several weeks. When she was unable to accept his invitation on one occasion, he felt subjected to the ridicule of his family, who witnessed his humiliation. He had not been able to envisage dating girls again until recently, almost 10 years later.

C. has dreamt that his "left side is unused," the only glimmering for a long while that he possessed some hidden, undiscovered potentialities for change. In therapy, despite his productivity and quite considerable insight, he was for a prolonged period reluctant, or simply too paralyzed or terrified, to translate this into action, since this signified leaving mother. Though in childhood C. never experienced conscious resentment regarding his mother, massive anger and disgust, as well as fear of annihilation regarding women, eventually emerged during therapy. Of interest was the unfolding of his awareness of mother's infantilization of him, of her castration of his father, and the gradual recognition of father as a more solid and differentiated person.

For C., change proved painstaking, halting, and laborious. He literally had to learn to walk, that is, to be guided

---

[1] Freud (1924) suggested that in feminine masochism in men, the fantasies that lead to masturbation have to do with situations in which one is beaten or degraded. Freud believed the masochist desires to be regarded as a small, helpless, dependent, or naughty child.

through the various developmental phases, in acquiring ego strength as well as social and adaptive skills. I had to help in creating bridges for him between home or therapy and the outside world.

PATIENT D.

D., 29, a tall, good-looking man of Jewish–Congregationalist, upper-middle-class parents and the eldest of two children, came to New York to seek therapy and maintain some distance from his recently widowed mother. He felt he "couldn't think in a straight line," had become insomniac, and experienced difficulties in holding a job. D. attended an Ivy League school, but despite his intelligence, he graduated at the bottom of his class.

D. had always been deeply conflicted regarding his mother, still an extremely attractive woman. He described her on the one hand as cold, seductive, "mean, hard, cruel, scared to death of her, came up here to get away from her, once dreamt she was a monster or a mannequin." On the other hand, the patient had worshipped his mother as "sweet and virginal" and fondly remembers she would read him fairy tales. Predominantly, though, he perceived her as phallic and masculine, as the powerful parent. She would mechanically punish him with a stick when she considered him naughty and prepared him for this in advance. He felt he "enjoyed" these situations because they manifested interest or attention on mother's part. Furthermore, his mother regularly and methodically administered enemas in an obvious power struggle with D. over toileting; here he felt degraded, though utterly compliant.

The children were reared by maids; D.'s fondest memories are of his Negro mammy. Yet, if his mother was off on a simple errand, D. often feared she might not return home, and frequently felt abandoned by her. Only in the event of illness could mother be depended upon to be solicitous or caring; D. suffered from asthma at a very early age.

He believed his parents definitely favored his sister, four years younger than he, whom he considered dazzlingly beautiful and more highly endowed. He considered himself ugly, repulsive, "bleary" and effeminate as a child. He remembered a vivid dream where "everyone will pounce on me, throw rocks, be against me."

D. perceived his father as loud, bombastic, bullying, "dark" (D. and his mother are blond); his father never played with him and was rarely home. Yet D. could somehow "trust" him to a greater extent than his mother in that he was more direct and predictable, less covert and enigmatic.

While riding his horse, the father was thrown and proved unable to extricate himself from a hazardous and vulnerable position. He suffered a severely broken leg that did not heal for many years. During this period, spanning the patient's ninth to sixteenth years, the father seemed both irascible and helpless, more inaccessible than ever to D., reinforcing his image of mother as the powerful parent. Also of interest is the fact D. had never acknowledged his Jewishness on the paternal side; he was informed his father belonged to the Jewish faith only following his death.

D. remembers he was an excellent student in elementary school, though his performance declined in the fourth grade, synchronizing with the birth of another sibling. He recalls a serious and painful arm injury at age 12 that lingered for one year; this was incurred during a fight with a classmate. Following this, D. avoided physical encounters and suffered feelings of impotence and emasculation. He did not, or could not, play ball with the other boys. Painting was his passion. After high school, he had a number of affairs with older women. Though he acquired sexual competence, he felt like "a gigolo or lackey."

When D. was 22, his father died of heart failure. Upon graduating from college a year later, the patient entered medical school, presumably to carry on the family tradition or to appease mother. His talents, more artistic than academic, focused particularly on painting. After a year of medical school and a newspaper job that he lost, D. felt: "If I try hard for anything, I won't get it. Or something will take me away from it. Or something terrible will happen." Should he complete a particular goal or project, he felt he would surely die. Feeling his mother's immense disapproval, D. left home to come to New York where he began therapy. Currently, he considers himself a failure, vacillates regarding his work orientation, is making tentative overtures towards encompassing both artistic and more conventionally professional goals, and, surprisingly, is managing both.

D.'s initial relationships with girls after coming to New York, though sexually somewhat successful, were essentially tentative and distant. He feared rejection and he himself rejected others. There seemed a greater emancipation from his mother, however, especially after he decided to refuse further financial assistance from her.

D.'s marriage has been damaged by a considerable degree of mutual competitiveness. The patient is becoming aware that this occurs because he views his wife in terms of ancient attitudes regarding his sister and mother. He hates her attractiveness, her need to be the center of attention, and feels she outdistances him in work.

PATIENT E.

E., transferring from another therapist, entered therapy with me because of her tendency to be involved in repetitively unrewarding, heterosexual situations.

E., 36, is the second oldest in a family of six. Her father, a lawyer, and a very learned, strict, cold, religious, critical, punitive man, would frequently yell and shout at her. Her earliest memory is of her father administering a spanking. Her mother generally sought to carry out the father's restrictions. It appears that E.'s mother performed routine physical ministrations but showed a minimum of attention or interest beyond this, unless the patient were ill. E. recalls that her mother occasionally made affectional overtures, but that she, E., kept her mother at a distance. The patient was considered weak, pale, sickly, and was prone to painful skin eruptions, fainting, headaches, and presumably to vaginal discharges, which the mother tended.

In the family constellation, E. found herself wedged in between two "brilliant" siblings, an older sister and younger brother, both outdistancing her intellectually, i.e., in terms of formal or academic learning. Her sister was ostensibly more self-sufficient and decorous than she. E. remembered that she, herself, was tomboyish; mechanically oriented; inclined more to abilities in art, music, and gym; and manifested reading and memory difficulties. She was punished for forgetting; she generally felt stupid, bad, deviant. Her mother would convey the feeling that someone who couldn't study was a "shame to the family" and would exclaim, "What will I do with her!" She inevitably sought to have E. perform some "useful" task. Work always acquired more importance than play in their household. Whenever E. heard her name, she wondered, "What did I do wrong?"

E. never displayed overt rebelliousness. In her preoccupation with religion, she felt her "goodness" triumphed over the evil of others. Not until she left home at age 18 to study at a music school in a nearby town where she remained for four years, did she attempt to realize her capacities. After this, she found work in a neighboring city.

Wishing to be attractive as a woman was at first taboo. In her mid-twenties, E. met and had an affair with a young man and corresponded with him for two years after he left for Europe. When she went abroad at his suggestion to live with him, she discovered he was involved with another woman. Nevertheless, she continued the relationship and would see him on "alternate" days, for some time afterward. Following this affair she began having masturbatory fantasies where she imagined herself being raped. Ever since, indeed until recently, she has chosen unavailable, manipulative, or sadistic partners in a succession of heterosexual relationships. She feels victimized and abused and complains and cries helplessly.

E. often acquiesces to sexual encounters though she may dislike her partner. She hates herself afterwards, feeling frustrated and resentful. Frequently, in describing her sexual feelings, she perceives the male as imprisoning, as holding her down so that she has no movement or mobility; she is unable to assert her wishes. This appears to go back to the bullying she received from her father and brothers: E. recalls a play experience in which her brother "bound" her. She is more sexually stimulated when in forbidden or complicated heterosexual situations.

The patient appears to relate to too great an extent on the level of physical exchanges with men, disregarding, or being unaware of, interpersonal nuances. Two previous therapists with whom she remained for long periods, both male, were preoccupied with bodily processes: one was a "body manipulator," who merely seemed to reinforce her dissociated focus on her body; the other was a person who believed, and convinced her, that a so-called zen macrobiotic diet would cure all. Following this latter "therapy," E. became ill and almost died. In her transference attitudes concerning her present analyst, E., perceiving me as a parent or sister figure, sought to elicit reactions from me indicating she was not competent or intelligent by acting inept or forgetful. Her sister is a university professor whom she places on a pedestal and relates to as though she were much older. E. often appears naïve and childlike in her questions and perceptions. She tends to behave as others expect her to, is unaware of any clear sense of self, and claims she enjoys situations only with or for someone else. She is puzzled when questioned as to what *she* might want for herself.

At work, her immediate supervisor is a younger, though fairly aggressive, woman, who more frequently than not asks the patient to go out and fetch her coffee, stockings, or what have you. The patient has complied, though with covert resentment. Again, it is difficult for her to communicate (let alone know) her own feelings in such situations.

When she began therapy about one and a half years ago, she had been briefly seeing a rather disturbed, divorced man, father of three children, who informed her that he had attempted suicide twice and had been hospitalized during a breakdown. She felt she was in love with him, principally because she had experienced orgasm with him. He promptly dropped her. Despite this, she pursued him. At a later casual meeting, he exhibited nude pictures of his current girl friend. She regarded this as sick but could feel no hatred or bitterness.

Currently E. sees a man who cares a good deal for her. Though she initially attested to little sexual responsiveness, she is gradually becoming aware of her past needs for excitement, complication, and rejection in order to feel sexually aroused. She has remained in the current relationship, however, and is beginning to enjoy the genuine friendliness and tenderness of this man. She does feel, though, that the relationship will not last, that the man will lose interest in her. For the first time she has managed to communicate

some degree of assertiveness at work when she feels over-
burdened or manipulated by her supervisor, or with her boy
friend when it might be appropriate. She is better able to
accept her boy friend's occasional remonstrances or spontaneous anger without permitting this to completely
demolish her. Furthermore, she is awakening to her hitherto modulated, but quite marked, needs for achievement and
accomplishment, without feeling this as shameful or masculine.

V. Developmental Patterns in Masochistic Behavior

Central trends in the clinical material[1] may best be summarized by referring back to the first question raised at the end of Chapter I: What are the unique characteristics in one's life history, particularly in the parent–child or family entity that make imperative the recourse to masochistic behavior?

Ambivalency patterns inherent in the early mother–infant relationship are crucial in initiating masochistic

---

[1] This summary is based on the foregoing clinical reports and data gleaned from other patients in analysis with me, as well as from clinical illustrations culled from the literature.

behavioral patterns. It is fairly well established that the child requires a durable, sustained, affectional tie with the mother figure for optimal development of all growth processes. That an affirmative relationship with mother is crucial for physical survival has of course been decisively shown in Spitz's (1944) studies on hospitalism in infants, as well as in the work of Bowlby (1966), regarding institutional children, and others, concerning normal and disturbed children (Ribble, 1943; Brody, 1956; Winnicott, 1965; Escalona, 1968).

"Imprinting," an early experience during which the young form a strong, social attachment to a mother-object, prevails in every social species particularly those in which there are extended periods of parental care. The critical period for humans, in Hess's (1962) view, extends from six weeks to six months. This may be too definite a delineation. Of interest in the experimental studies, however, is the finding that painful stimulation creates an enhancement of the effectiveness of the imprinting experience, should this occur in the phase of "maximum imprintability."

Lichtenstein (1961) suggests that the concept "imprinting" be used for the unconscious, symbiotic communication between mother and child, in which there is an incorporation of the unconscious, negative expectations of the mother. The manner in which mother touches, holds, and warms the child, the way in which some senses are stimulated and others not, forms a "stimulus cast" of mother's unconscious. One might also think in terms of an introjection of "patterned relationships" (Grinker, 1957), evolving from nuances of gratification, as well as frustration, the latter leading to suffering and pain. The self may then literally become the frustrating mother.

Bieber (1966) describes the masochistic defense patterns in a three-and-a-half-year-old child prior to treatment. Whenever the mother physically punished her daughter, the child would threaten to, or actually would, harm herself by banging her head or hands on solid objects, sometimes leading to hematomata, or by burning her hand on a radiator or open flame. In so doing, for the most part, she warded off physical punishment. Her mother, resentful and retaliative regarding the daughter's pseudotriumph, did not, however, completely omit corporal beatings. The child, in turn, expanded her maneuvers. For example, when her physician accidentally gagged her with a tongue depressor during a throat examination, she tore at the mucosa in her mouth, preventing further probing. Thus, self-inflicted punishment deflects or controls injury or hostility considered hurtful or threatening. Though ultimately maladaptive, the masochistic structure is reinforced because of its initial adaptive implications.

Two categories of parental psychopathology leading to masochistic behavior are delineated by Bieber: hostility and ambivalence toward the child, and the acting out of masochism through the child. This latter reflects a parental anticipation of injury—possibly connected to a fear of having a valued child—that may be externalized in such a way that the child is inundated with oversolicitous concern or restrictions. Or the parent, by identifying with his child, seeks to gratify thwarted aspirations via the success of his child, behaving as neurotically concerning his offspring's achievements as toward his own.

Clinical findings suggest it is of decisive importance that the child cling to the parent to maintain some means of contact, even though the attention or care given may be negative or noxious,[1] since the danger of total abandonment is much greater. Unconsciously, the child feels his masochistic behavior is a means of placating his parents. Frequently he perpetuates the masochistic interplay by his provocativeness, eliciting rejection from the very person or persons from whom affection is sought, and thus catalyzing or accelerating the sadomasochistic cycle still further. Childhood experiences initiating such modes of interaction help to form a character structure that reflects the original, inappropriately nurturing, situation in later unsatisfactory transferences.

The mothers of our masochistic patients generally fluctuate radically in their ministrations during the oral or nursing period and beyond. On the one hand, they appear depriving, unempathic, unaffirming, frustrating, or rejecting. On the other, they may be anxiously or guiltily oversolicitous and infantilizing. Menaker (1942) describes her patient's fear of starving in relation to a neglectful, abandoning mother and the mother's subsequent overprotection of her daughter by literally spoonfeeding her until she was 10 years old. E. almost starved herself in obediently conforming to a therapist's macrobiotic diet, thereby reenacting a childhood situation. B. and C. have had lifelong struggles with alternately overeating and dieting, pointing to a conflict-ridden relationship with mother in the oral period. B. also has had a drinking problem.

Mothers of masochistic children may be perceived as pervasively guilt-provoking and undermining, alternately invasive and remote. They are heedful of physical

---

[1] Both C. and D. "enjoyed" parental beatings, since these engendered some degree of caring by otherwise unresponsive and ungiving parents. C., considered a "bag of garbage" by his mother when he was an infant, was so compliant that toilet training was completed before he was one year old.

needs but respond to them in a methodical fashion, offering a minimal amount of tactile communication or gratuitous attention. Marked sibling favoritism is experienced, reinforcing the sense of mother's absence or neglect. Traumatic deprivation might ensue as a result of constitutional predisposition or congenital activity pattern,[1] low frustration tolerance, abruptness of weaning, disciplinary measures concerning toilet training, masturbation, or normal exploratoriness.

In short, the parental ambivalence is weighted on the hostile side, the parent inflicting a sense of injury or ill treatment upon the child despite a pretext of caring. Severe and overt cruelty occur but are not the rule. This might be more pathognomonic of families where delinquent or psychopathic behavior patterns in children emerge.

The patients' mothers did not evince much joy or pleasure in their maternal role. At the same time, they wished to control their children's lives. They were invasive within, as well as outside, the home, frequently cutting off or circumscribing all other experiences and either directly or subtly forcing the child to do so himself.

Physical illness, tendency to accidents, or marked bodily-preoccupation seemed significant in the group and were used as a device to solicit or wrest mother's attention. Almost all of the patients manifested psychosomatic reactions at an early age; suffered headaches or asthma; were told they were repulsively thin, sallow, or ugly; or evidenced disfiguring skin eruptions. Spitz (1951), in seeking the etiological factors in children who manifest skin disorders during the first year of life, points to mothers who display considerable overt anxiety and who avoid touching their infants due to a marked degree of repressed hostility.

---

[1] A child with a "quiet" activity pattern (Malcove, 1945) might quite simply be ignored or understimulated.

In discussing the personality patterns of mothers of "moral masochists," Bromberg (1955) indicates that they present themselves as devoted, self-sacrificing, and solicitous, though their quite considerable narcissism and hostility negate this. They advocate and enforce repression of overt manifestations of sexual impulses, yet are at the same time sexually seductive. The parents act out the ambivalent feelings they unconsciously harbor towards a sibling or parent from their own childhood. They treat the child cruelly, seductively, and restrictively, interfering with the development of the child's ego and convincing the child he is most loved when suffering most. This leads to a search for suffering where love is what is desired.

In the later childhood of the patients, the mother figure continues to be seen as omniscient and powerful, endowed by the child with indomitable strength. By contrast, the child perceives himself as inordinately powerless, dependent, or helpless; evidences severe confusion concerning personal identification; and manifests a muted, weak sense of self.

Furthermore, the mothers generally assume the stance of martyr or victim. Despite this, they remain the powerful figure[1] at home. Father retains little prestige with the children and is excluded from decision making. Though in the early, oral stage, the nature of rapport between mother and infant is crucial, the relationship with the father, as well as the father's role in the entire family structure, assumes signi-

---

[1] B.'s mother seems the exception; her father is the authoritarian figure and her mother remained more child than wife or mother. Her displacement by the father in her maternal role has had insidious effects on B., as mentioned. Lidz (1957) has designated three varieties of marital constellation as potentially hazardous to optimal family integration : (1) a "man-dominated competitive axis," where the husband asserts male dominance to a pathological degree, undercutting mother's role with the children; (2) a "woman-dominated competitive

ficance quite early, as does the perception of the relationship between the parents.

Lidz (1957) states that the father is the leader of the family in "adaptive–instrumental" situations, while the mother has primacy in "integrative–expressive" areas. The mother's ability to be nurturant and secure in the mothering role cannot be separated from the support she gains from the father and his ability to share the child. Fathers who resent the intrusion of a child, express rivalry regarding the mother (true of B.'s father) feel competitive regarding the child (true of the fathers of patients C. and D.), or are exaggeratedly subservient or domineering, frequently participate in intrafamilial interactions leading to pathology in the patients.

Nydes (1963), on examining the family background of his "paranoid–masochistic" patients, suggests that it is the lack of rational, consistent parental authority, rather than the harsh experience of such authority, that is decisive. Frequently, in the case of his male patients, the mother is dominating and overprotective, while the father may be indifferent, detached, separated, or dead. Perhaps the absence for the male of a father figure who is both accepting and disciplining facilitates the notion that the "illusory infantile superego figure is, in fact, real." This might account for C.'s exaggeratedly brutish conception of his father, despite the father's lowly position in the family.

The fathers of the patients seemed bombastic, punitive, ridiculing, paranoid, or authoritarian or gave evidence of

---

axis," characterized by the wife's exclusion of a passive husband from leadership by constantly derogating him, resulting in his withdrawal from the situation in an effort to preserve his integrity; and (3) a "dual immature dependency axis," where there is mutual withdrawal of partners and dependency on parental families. These categories seem somewhat rigid or limited, though they are operationally helpful.

powerful physical strength in their impact on our patients as young children. Actually, only one, B.'s father, emerged as the undisputed authority at home. The others seemed essentially weak, childlike, or remote in terms of the alignment of power in the home, though this was not evident to the child in his early years. The marginal work situation of several fathers led to feelings of failure and impotence, that incurred the contempt of their wives and engendered in their children the fear of going beyond them.

In all the families, the parents displayed excessive dependency on their original family and incestuous or encapsulating attitudes concerning their children. Alternately, they completely rejected the parental role. Furthermore, though the parents of the patients were pathologically argumentative and at cross purposes, displayed mutual distrust, and showed practically no positive satisfactions in their marriages, they sought to establish a myth of harmony.

The patients, despite inherently superior intellectual capacities, underestimated their abilities, showed much difficulty in learning and intellectual areas, or reflected indecisiveness as regards career orientation. They remained in jobs below their training or ability or incommensurate with their interests. Few functioned in consonance with their potential or showed optimal levels of aspiration. According to Berliner (1947) the masochist may deny his intelligence, often to the point of "pseudo-debility."[1] Obviously, with such marginal accomplishments, these patients may be either placating or avoiding the contemptuousness of parents who expect them to be failures.[2]

---

[1] Berliner quotes one of his patients : "If I were clever, successful, lovable, I would make it impossible for my father to hate me. Then I would claim to be loved by him. He wishes to see me unlovable so that he can hate me. I therefore cannot be clever, lovable, and successful."
[2] A low level of aspiration is frequently, culturally induced in women.

Early oral frustrations handicap the integrated development of the child, interfering with optimal growth of ego skills. The sense of insufficiency and incompetence may be reinforced by the mother's excessive concern for the child in guise of oversolicitousness or overprotectiveness, making it more difficult for the child to assume an independent direction. These early deprivations are further entrenched by similar experiences in ensuing levels of development. Thus, from a fairly early age, the child both perceives and experiences his own inadequate functioning. This is facilitated by the mother's need to delineate or cherish his dependency and helplessness. In addition, the child identifies with her punitiveness.

Furthermore, the patients, by their masochism, may be punishing or spiting parents who have arbitrary expectations for them and whom they cannot otherwise confront. They may also be fearful of superseding an ineffectual or failure-oriented father.

Concerning techniques for handling aggression, a number of our patients rarely experienced conscious awareness of anger or rebelliousness in relation to their parents. Before therapy, they were good, conforming, muted children, never realizing that there could be alternative styles. They tended to channelize resentments in psychosomatic disorders, or they would resort to both self-aggrandizing and self-debasing fantasies and dreams, sexual or otherwise. Hostilities were generally projected onto others or onto impersonal forces. Marked dependency needs, occasionally of a parasitical, demanding sort, were pervasive.

Research on motivation and achievement using TAT responses with reference to women, points to a wish for failure or need to avoid success : For example, excellence is associated with loss of femininity, social rejection, personal or societal destruction, or some combination of these (Gornick, 1971).

Insofar as sexual differences concerning masochistic patterns are concerned, our female patients tended to feel victimized and abused by men, identifying with the mother's basic attitudes regarding her marital role. Alternately, they had themselves experienced some degree of rejection through the sadistic or detached attitudes of the father or father figures. From earliest infancy, the girl child needs the father in order to evolve a separate identity and to individuate from the mother. Most centrally, the relationship with the father facilitates her experience of herself as a female and helps her relate to others as a female (Forrest, 1966).

The female patients appeared unaware of their own provocativeness in heterosexual situations or of the underlying motivation for their choice of ineffectual or unavailable men, though harboring elaborate fantasies of retaliation and revenge. They displayed marked conflict regarding relationships with women as well: in feeling intimidated and invaded by female authority figures, in the ambivalent need for a close relationship with a mother figure, in their intense rivalries with girl friends, and in their expressions of role confusion. Also of interest is the fact that our female patients display a predominantly physical[1] approach to men. Perhaps they felt the physical modality to be the primary mode of eliciting male interest, though this could also be the expression of a longing for a primitive maternal, tactile intimacy. Yet, when participating in casual sexual experiences, the patients felt humiliated and degraded. In past relationships, all have required masochistic fantasies of rape or assault or a considerable degree of sheer sensation, rejection, or excitement to feel optimally aroused.

---

[1] Reich (1933) indicates that skin erotism is a crucial feature in masochism, related to fear of being alone or of losing contact with the love-object.

Our male patients have been markedly attached and erotically attracted to, as well as dominated by, phallic, seductive, overwhelming, or castrating mothers, the latter contemptuous of their husbands and rejecting their feminine role. Occasionally they became mother's confidante, usurping the father's role. These patients were eventually able in therapy to externalize their massive hostility and disgust regarding women, though their habitual attitudes regarding the mother were compliant, emasculated, submissive or overidealizing. Concerning the father, male patients frequently felt castrated or crushed. The central feeling is one of estrangement and distance, predominantly due to the mother cutting off the father in his paternal role by openly or obliquely ridiculing him or wallowing in her suffering. This results in insuperable obstacles in the son's identification process, i.e., in his assumption of a vigorous male role and in his heterosexual adaptation.

Thus, in the family background of masochistic patients, there appears to be a pattern of an angry, critical, or undermining father who is, however, frequently seen as markedly inadequate and threatened by the mother; linked with a depriving, infantilizing, overidealized, subtly dominating mother, herself mother-attached or with submerged dependency needs.

Perhaps the tenuous self-image noted in our patients may have to do with the introjection of parental ambivalence in the process of their early identification with a parent and with the depreciated images for identification presented by the devaluation of one parent by another. Framo (1965) suggests that introjects have to do not only with a one-to-one relationship with the mother and father as individuals but with the pattern of the marital relationship, with the parents' conception of their respective roles, and with the emotional mother- and father-surrogates, which may include siblings. The entire family matrix—its emotions, codes, myths, language, and cognitive style may frequently be introjected.

An analysis of masochistic formations in the patients encompasses the following premises:

1. Oral and tactile insufficiency or deprivation is generally deeply embedded in, and characteristic of, the mother–infant relationship and seems to derive from the mother's inconsistent, ambivalent, alternatingly withholding and engulfing attitudes.

2. Optimal emotional or libidinal availability of the mother is denied or irregular during the ensuing, critical growth periods. That is, early masochistic predilections set up a developmental imbalance that continues to reverberate in succeeding periods—anal, phallic, and genital—so that there may be sharp dissonances in the optimal growth of ego functions.

3. Masochistic self-devaluations, imprinted by incorporation of the unconscious, negative expectations of the mother, serve as a defensive structure. The intent is to accommodate the mother by ego-constriction and failure. Any awareness of the deprivation and meagerness of the maternal relationship is masked, and a distortedly benign image of the parent is maintained with particular vigilance. All expression of conscious hostility is avoided for fear of separation or loss.

4. The sadomasochistic interplay with mother may be perpetuated by transferences to parent-surrogates and others, the better to hold onto a primitive tie with the mother and avoid the feared separation.

5. The nature of the relationship with the father, from early infancy through adolescence, is crucial in setting up masochistic formations, as are the implications of

father's role as marital partner as well as his and the mother's role in the entire family and social structure.

Motivated by fear of emotional abandonment, the patient, in incorporating the negation and criticalness of the parent, seeks to avoid the implications of deprivation, unwantedness, invasiveness, and guilty engulfment as well as concomitant anxieties and resentments. Masking the ambivalent parent as unambiguously benign, self-devaluation serves to preserve some tie or manner of relationship with the parent and is perhaps necessary for survival. Regarding the patients described here, this is reinforced when the mother's malevolence in the nurturing role and the father's distance or authoritarian punitiveness lies within the context of marital or familial fragmentation.

VI. Differential Diagnosis

How do masochistic mechanisms differ from depressive, obsessional, or paranoid patterns of behavior, often confused with aspects of masochistic suffering?

The tendency to regard masochism as a specific disorder is a residue of the Kraepelinian period when sexual deviations were investigated as separate categories, not necessarily related to other personality disturbances. Hoch (1959) indicates masochism may occur in neurosis, psychopathy, depression, and schizophrenia. In effect, masochism can only be evaluated in such a framework. To Hoch the fundamental question is: "Do we have a psychopathological entity which can be explained dynamically in a similar way in all persons . . . or merely phenomenologically similar features of which the causation is not the same."

Since genetically masochistic patterns are principally attributable to early oral deprivation and trauma—not necessarily to the vicissitudes of the oedipal period as Freud would have it—does one then link them with psychotic or depressive states? Or with perversions and impulse disorders as Fenichel (1945) does? Is one to discard diagnostic categories or view them instead with a greater degree of fluidity and permeability? There is considerable confusion regarding these questions in the literature.

DEPRESSION AND MASOCHISM

Numerous writers connect and often confuse masochistic with depressive states: Fenichel (1945) suggests that depressive patients seek to influence or coerce significant figures in the environment to "restore their lost self-esteem." Frequently they attempt to "captivate their objects in a way characteristic for masochistic characters" by demonstrating their suffering, by suggesting that others are responsible for their misery, or by blackmailing them into giving affection.

According to Reich (1933), to the extent that oral demands play a central role in masochism, they determine depressive tendencies.

Berliner (1958) indicates that moral masochism and depression are linked as follows: In the process of introjection, the rejecting partner, along with a general ambience of suffering, become constituents of the superego; the "libidinization" renders the trauma ego syntonic, protecting one from an overly severe degree of suffering, though it still does not heal the narcissistic wound. Throughout life the superego compels the person to "relive and re-enact" the original trauma, as noted in the unpleasurable situations experienced by, and actively sought after by the masochist. Like the melancholic, the masochist "hangs on so to speak to a breast which is not there, and which he has to repudiate when it could be there symbolically."

"The depressive maneuver is similar to the masochistic defense in many ways," states Salzman (1962). In describing depression, he points to the angry rebukes and hostile recriminations, along with the self-derogation and denial, expressed by his patients. Ultimately suicide may occur, finalizing self-denial and hopeless despair. The "depressive maneuver" is a defense against the loss or supposed loss of a person or value highly meaningful to the individual's integration. Viewed as a process of repair, there is an attempt to replace or make up for these losses by a variety of devices, among them the masochistic defense, in which the individual insists that he cannot live unless these lost objects are restored. The masochist, according to Salzman, "demands that he get what he is entitled to, never admitting that he has lost anything or that he needs anything."

With a weakening of masochistic equilibrium, via threatened or actual loss of love, there may be an impoverishment of defensive and adaptive ego functions, in addition to a disappearance of the crucial controls usually afforded by the defensive and synthesizing mechanisms of the ego (Brenman, 1952). Infantile need and rage emerge more sharply, externalizing the "well-known extortionist demands for love," from marked self-deprecation to suicidal gestures. Should decompensation continue further without a successful suicide, there is a continuation of the imperative infantile need for nurturance, as well as ill-concealed rage or actual destructiveness, which may eventuate in psychotic depression, demonstrating the "emotional blackmail" seen in the hospitalized masochistic character who has decompensated. Beck (1967) was able to show that patients suffering from severe depressive illness had more "masochistic" signs in their dream content than patients less severely depressed.

Nacht and Racamier (1960) note that depression resembles moral masochism inasmuch as a "defensive exchange of aggressive behavior" is involved, but depression is distinct from masochism in that the relationship is less evolved, the separation of subject and object less complete. Frequently, depression occurs when a masochistic relationship or situation has ended or has been broken off. Perhaps the individual, no longer able to tolerate abuse at the hands of another, inflicts suffering on himself by "interiorizing the sadistic object." This prevents the person from being without the "suffering necessary to his defensive equilibrium" and avoids the loss of a tie with another, which, even if painful or deleterious, was considered a close and necessary bond of love. The authors liken depression to an acute crisis of moral masochism. In masochism, object and subject are experienced and postulated as existing independently of each other. This is not the case in depression, they state, since the object attacked has been unconsciously introjected by the patient. Should the depressive destroy himself, it is as though he were destroying the incorporated object.

Viewing the clinical manifestations of aggression according to the degree of organization of the defense mechanism protecting the ego, Nacht and Racamier find that depression resides between psychosomatic aggression and moral masochism.

OBSESSIVE–COMPULSIVE NEUROSIS AND MASOCHISM

In "Instincts and Their Vicissitudes," Freud (1915b) indicates that obsessional neuroses reflect a "turning upon the subject's self without the attitude of passivity toward another." Furthermore, "self-torment and self-punishment have arisen from the desire to torture, but not masochism."

Fenichel (1945), discussing obsessional states, suggests that the ego, in defending itself against the demands of the sadistic superego, may use a "counter-sadistic rebellion" as well as submission, or both attitudes simultaneously. Occasionally, the ego suffers acts of expiation and even torture to "an astonishing degree." Moral masochism appears as adjunct to the sadism of the superego; this submission is performed in hope of using it as license for later instinctual freedom. The ego's need for punishment is, in general, subordinated to a need for forgiveness and is accepted as a necessary means for avoiding the pressure of the superego. Such a need for punishment on the part of a compulsive ego may become condensed with masochistic sexual wishes.

Since an ambivalent dependency on a sadistic superego and the necessity to obliterate unbearable guilt tension are the most frequent precursors to suicide, one may ask why suicide is so rare in obsessive compulsion. Obsessive–compulsive neurotics, in contrast to depressives, do not involve the libido of the individual as totally in the conflict between ego and superego. A considerable portion of the patient's object relationships is thus preserved. Perhaps the regressive distortion or sadistic nature of these object relationships help to channel massive hostility against others, so that there is simply not as much need to direct quantities of aggression against oneself.

Berliner (1947) believes that since symptoms are mixed and neurotic conditions tend to blend, masochistic and obsessive traits might inhere in the same person. Specifically, masochism and compulsion neurosis may be similar insofar as self-deprecating attitudes are concerned. The prevailing notion that in masochism one deals with need for punishment and feelings of guilt about one's sadistic impulses applies actually to compulsion neuroses. Differential conditions, he proposes, are as follows: Masochism evolves from oral erotism and is the "libidinal reaction to another person's sadism," whereas compulsion neurosis derives from anal erotism and "from one's own sadism and fear of its consequences," though masochistic motivations may be present. Further, the masochist has a weak ego, is dependent, love seeking, and forms a strong transference in therapy, whereas the compulsion neurotic evidences a strong ego supported by anal aggressiveness, is stubborn, often negativistic, and shows little need for love. The need for love may be repressed or warded off by isolation, which is presumably not the case in the masochist. Finally, the compulsion neurotic displays difficulties in forming a transference. According to Berliner, the basic unconscious idea in the compulsion neurotic is, "What have I done?" The aim is to avoid anxiety. The masochist on the other hand asks, "What has been done to me?" His aim, to gain love. The compulsion neurotic is "paying an imaginary debt," not knowing what the real debt was; the masochist "is presenting an old unpaid bill for affection."

MASOCHISM AND PARANOID MECHANISMS

Nydes (1963) suggests that the paranoid and masochistic characters are closely related "if perceived as two strategies in a futile and conflicted struggle for control with an 'omnipotent will'." The masochistic character apparently rejects power "for the sake of love;" the paranoid character rejects love "for the sake of power." Love is equated with submission to the love-object, power with enforcing submission from another. According to Nydes, the sadomasochistic character should be termed paranoid-masochistic. The paranoid orientation involves identification as the victim whose cause is aggressively supported. A sadistic orientation relates more to identification with the aggressor, which seems to be a retaliative measure regarding suffering actually experienced.

Paranoia is perceived by Bak (1946) as "delusional masochism." Regression from sublimated homosexuality to masochism is, according to his view, an essential feature of the paranoid reaction. By withdrawal of love, the ego protects itself from masochistic threats coming from the id. There is an increase of hostility, hatred of the love-object, and sadistic fantasies of being mistreated. Projection of sadism, that is, thoughts of being injured and persecuted, gratify the original masochistic desires for castration, beating, and abuse by the father.

The ego aligns itself "on the side of sadism;" masochism serves to reestablish object cathexis and to hinder further defusion. The antagonistic hypercathexis of the two psychic agencies is an attempt to achieve equilibrium. Depending on economic factors, the outcome may be flight, murder, suicide, or subsiding of the tension and cessation of the attack. Megalomania seems to be a later development when quantities of masochistic cathexis are further withdrawn.

Aside from the masochistic implications in paranoid structures, the entire schizophrenic syndrome presents a florid spectrum of masochistic behavior, stemming from the self-destructive activities in childhood schizophrenia to the self-mutilation in agitated states or death-in-life manifestations of catatonic mechanisms.

Early parent–child relationships, especially insofar as degrees of closeness (symbiosis) or distance (separation) from the mother are concerned, might prove crucial in approaching the problems of differential diagnosis.

In the childhood of schizophrenics there is a lack of emotional differentiation of mother and child, as well as an abnormally low tolerance for frustration in the child. According to Mahler (1952):

The reality ties of the infant devolve upon the early delusional fusion with the mother; panic reactions set in at those points of the physiological and psychological maturation process at which separateness from the mother must be perceived and faced.

Mahler suggests that constitutional factors, as well as parental psychopathology, are etiological factors. Where parental pathology plays a role, the adult apparently accepts the child only as a "quasi-vegetative" being, an appendage to the parent's body.

Furthermore, in schizophrenic children the integration of good and bad mother-images—as well as clear differentiation of representations of the part-objects in the outside versus the part-images of the self—has been defective. At the point where fear of reengulfment, a fear amounting to fear of dissolution of identity, meets with its opposite, separation panic, the two overwhelm the ego. Thus, the integration and unlocking of "couplings" of scattered part-image representations of the self and object are prevented, creating regression to the stage in which unneutralized libido and aggression were vested in the symbiotic system within the child's delusional reality. Here the real mother ceases to exist as a separate entity. The introjected split objects permeate the psychotic child's world.

In a study by Fromm-Reichmann, *et al.* (1959), the mothers of depressive patients were described as thriving on the early, almost complete dependency of infancy, whereas the increasing independence of early childhood proved threatening to them. The previously loving mother abruptly emerges as a harsh and punitive figure at approximately the end of the first year. The child may thus experience difficulty integrating the early "good," later "bad" mother into a total, unitary parent image. Similar complexities confront all children. However, this split in attitude concerning authority, eventually resolved in some, persists with the depressive. Thus an important authority may be regarded as the source of all good things when he is pleased and alternately may be considered tyrannical and punitive unless placated by good behavior.

As long as the patient cannot tolerate the notion that one object gives both satisfaction and disappointment, he will be depressive. He protects himself against ambivalence by splitting his object representation into the image of the perfect, idealized object, which has nothing to do with the complementary representation of the bad object. The real object is measured against a gratifying ideal of perfection, to which it must immediately conform or be rejected as bad.

In the depressive, the incorporation of another person for purposes of filling an inner emptiness and, of acquiring a borrowed self-esteem is different from the lack of ego boundaries in the schizophrenic. The latter is in danger of losing his ego; the depressive is threatened by object loss, since he habitually employs the object to bolster his ego weakness. Object relations in the depressive are indeed distorted. However, by complaining or blaming the frustrating object, the depressive is—precisely because of this agitated activity in the service of his own salvation—defended against loss of ego.

There is little to affirm Nacht and Racamier's view that the masochistic personality is necessarily more individuated in regard to separation from the partner. The prevalent belief, rather, is that in the masochistic personality, oral fixations and frustrations are marked. All too frequently there is a merging of child with parent, and later of masochistic adult with sadistic partner.

One might say that in masochism, as compared to depression, the mother, despite her ambivalency, tends to be regarded benignly as "good," inasmuch as awareness of one's hostility could create too threatening an estrangement. Retaining the "good image of the mother on a preambivalent level, the ego of the child, masochistically and at its own expense, tries to establish and maintain a primitive object relationship. In this way the masochistic ego reaction serves as a defense against a psychosis" (Menaker, 1953). The projection of the mother's omnipotence and the ensuing derogation of the self functions as a "mechanism of psychological survival." Despite the merging with the mother, enough ego development has occurred in the child to create a perception of his own ego as separate from his mother's. In short, should the mother be totally fused with the child's ego, a psychotic confusion of identity would result.

In summary, in the schizophrenic there is lack of emotional separation and differentiation of mother and child. The schizophrenic alternates between desiring to fuse with the "good" mother and avoiding reengulfment with the "bad" mother. When aggressive impulses predominate, emotional states may arise in the patient in which love and hate or good and bad objects cannot be separated and are experienced as mixed up or confused.

The depressive finds fusing the early "good" with later "bad" mother-image troublesome. The depressive has not accepted the bad mother as his fate. He vacillates between phases in which he combats the bad mother and those in which he feels reunited with the good mother.

The masochist regards the mother as pervasively

"good," for awareness of resentment would create too threatening an estrangement. In a sense, the masochist remains in a lifelong symbiotic, sadomasochistic relationship with the undermining parent or later adult partner or parent-surrogate, who for purposes of the individual's own self-preservation, is viewed as benign or "good."

VII. The Role of Sadism or Aggression in Masochism

What are the techniques employed by masochistic personalities for handling aggression? Is the masochist both sadist and sufferer, that is, sadomasochistic? Or is this a misleading merging of two distinct entities?

The category sadomasochism was initially formulated by Freud in his early writings on sexual aberrations where he suggested that sadistic and masochistic components may accompany the sexual drive or may comprise a "fixation of precursory sexual aims." Sadism, he felt, comprises the active, masochism the passive, component. In this context sadism is viewed as emanating from the presumed sexual aggressiveness of men, their need to conquer or "overcome the resistance" of the female; Freud emphasized that he is not merely referring to predatory or violent attitudes but rather to the humiliation or abuse of the sexual partner. Most centrally, in his construct both forms of the perversion inhere in the same person, one or the other emerging in accordance with the prevailing sexual behavior. In short, "a sadist is always at the same time a masochist." Though the active or passive component may predominate, these components are rather murkily linked to masculinity and femininity. In his later division of the instincts into life and death urges, Freud still adhered to the notion that sadism not channelized into actual life is turned against the self, thereby setting up a secondary masochism. After Freud, the dual terminology delineating sadomasochistic behavioral trends or personality patterns, lingered.

There are many puzzling features in Freud's theory of "sadism turned round upon the self." According to Freud, should one assume a masochistic role in a particular situation, one could presumably shift to a sadistic role in another context. It seems questionable, however, that roles may be reversed with the ease Freud suggests.

Also, Freud seemed unable to distinguish levels of meaning regarding motivational pattern or factors of individual difference in the expression of sadistic or aggressive traits. He further failed to differentiate healthy, normal aggression,[1] that is, needs for mastery, activity, or assertiveness from irrational, destructive, vengeful aggression, and employed the term sadistic for both. Largely ignored in his

---

[1] Solnit (1972) suggests that after separation from the mother due to illness, infant aggression appears as a healthy drive that is activated and revitalized by resumption of good mothering. Affectionate, contented behavior, a fusion of libidinal and aggressive states, accompanies the reemergence of aggressive drive activity.

writings are the many-faceted interactions of situation and character leading to aggressive behavior.

In this study, masochism and sadism are not perceived as necessarily occurring within the same person. Sadomasochism, masochism as the turning of sadism in upon the self, are not equated. It is my contention that masochistic[1] trends differ from sadistic trends in terms of the person's intrapsychic dynamics and character structure. Both entities evidence self-harming, as well as aggressive, components but these have qualitatively different nuances insofar as the relationship to self and others are concerned. Since masochism and sadism are so inextricably intertwined, however, in specific interpersonal constellations, a brief discussion of the concept of sadism, rarely explored in the literature, seems indicated.

Krafft-Ebing (1900), who first described sadism, considered it a pathological elaboration of a normal, aggressive component of male sexuality. He also indicated sadism could easily be transferred from one excitatory constellation to another. Components of the attack pattern of behavior, for example, could be incorporated into the sexual matrix. Once the association between sexuality and cruelty are fixated, one modality can elicit the other.

Freud's successive theories on masochism and the linkage with sadism in a seeming unity of opposites have been extensively delineated, with stress on the masochistic dimension. In his earliest writings, Freud was preoccupied with libido and attempted to clarify its role in neurotic conflicts. The emphasis on libido served to relegate aggression to a minor role. Aggressive impulses were described only with reference to sexual aberration and to sequential stages of psychosexual development.

---

[1] Freud indicated that masochistic fantasies rarely approximate the brutality of those that are sadistic.

Both Freud (1905) and Abraham (1948), in elaborating the psychosexual levels of development, indicated that sadism accompanies oral and anal phases. Oral sadism is associated with oral erotism and is evidenced in unconscious fantasies of biting[1] or devouring and the derivatives of these fantasies in conscious behavior. In this stage, the infant may destroy what he appropriates, suck the object dry or try to take everything into himself. The aims of oral incorporation often assume a sadistic character, particularly following the ambivalent phase. That is, when a conception of objects has evolved, there may be a connection of ideas of incorporation with sadism, especially in the event that definite frustrations have occurred. Schizophrenia—the addictions, masochistic reactions, and the manic–depressive cycle—present manifestations of fixation at the oral level. Cannibalistic fantasies are frequently demonstrable in the delusions of melancholia.

The peak of aggression is attained during the anal stage when sadistic urges to hurt and dominate others are noted for their frequency and intensity. Anal sadism accompanies

---

[1] Kacera (1959) indicates that in dentition, the very activities by which tension has hitherto been removed, sucking and gnawing, provide more pain and tension; a link is thus established between satisfaction of libidinal and aggressive drives on the one hand and painful experiences on the other. This experience, which is regularly evoked during normal teeth eruption, can be looked upon as the key situation for the origin of primary masochism : its physiological, organic foundation. Erikson (1950) suggests that a social dilemma is added to the physical one. That is, where breast feeding lasts into the biting stage, it is necessary for the infant to learn how to continue sucking without biting, so that mother may not withhold the nipple in pain or anger. It is at this point in the individual's early history that Erikson points to an "evil dividedness" where anger against the gnawing teeth, anger against the withholding mother, and anger with one's impotent anger all result in a dramatic experience of sadistic and masochistic confusion leaving the impression that "once upon a time one destroyed one's unity with a maternal matrix."

anal erotism and is subsumed in unconscious fantasies of beating, exploding, torturing, destroying, dirtying, and so on, and the derivative of these fantasies in conscious behavior. The "pinching-off" of feces may be viewed as a sadistic act. Later in life, persons may be regarded as the feces previously were. There are also physiological reasons for linking anal erotism with ambivalence and bisexuality, i.e., the child may treat the feces in a contradictory manner, expelling the matter from the body, or retaining it as if it were a loved object. Conflicts regarding toilet training may be expressed in feelings of omnipotence, power, or stubbornness regarding the mother, in giving or not giving the feces, in letting go or holding on. Characterologically, the child may be clinging, possessive, quarrelsome, tormenting,[1] provocative, untidy. This stage may therefore become a battle for autonomy. The close association of anal erotism and a specific constellation of character traits subsumed in obsessive–compulsive neuroses convinced Freud that regression to the anal–sadistic level is central to this disorder.

Insofar as sadistic implications of the phallic phase are concerned, Gero (1962) indicated the pervasiveness of sadomasochistic fantasies and drive patterns where the father is projected as the intrusive attacker, the mother as sufferer and victim,[2] and the sexual act as a cruel, painful, bloody, yet exciting and pleasurable event. Aggressive phallic fantasies may also have to do with feelings of omnipotence regarding urethral prowess or may accompany masturbation. Competition, envy, and need for intactness are characterological traits originating in this phase.

---

[1] At this pregenital level it is not so much hate but aggressive love that threatens to destroy the object; for example, pet animals or favorite toys frequently have to be rescued from the child whose aggression invariably accompanies the affection bestowed (A. Freud, 1949).

[2] Mother may also be perceived as incorporative in a spidery way.

Still another manifestation of the phallic period is the projection of the "phallic mother," who, according to Brunswick (1940), is endowed with the authority to restrict, prohibit, and command, and, until the subsequent depreciation because of her castration, is not only active and intrusive, but omnipotent as well. Brunswick feels the concept of a phallic mother emerges after the realization occurs that women do not possess a penis, i.e., it serves as a compensatory fantasy to assuage the child's fear of losing his penis.

Finally, in the oedipal stage, rivalry with the same-sex parent for love of the opposite-sex parent may lead to death wishes toward the hated rival. During the oedipal period individual drive patterns are restructured; sadistic acts continue to be identified with the role of the male, the cruel attacker who inflicts pain and injury. The masochistic destiny is designated as the woman's role. Woman endures the cruel attack and finds pleasure in yielding and submitting to the male. Gero (1962) essentially agrees with Freud, who also viewed sadism and masochism in the context of bisexual organization and felt they provided a basic definition for the difference in male and female roles.

The final stage of psychosexual maturation is reached by way of relinquishing oedipal objects. This involves diminution of ambivalent feelings toward the same-sex parent and identification with the parent in gender role. Thus the boy identifies with his father who, in the child's fantasy, threatens to castrate or banish him in retaliation for the child's oedipal wish to displace him. By internalizing the father's threat, the child defends against, and controls, his incestuous and parricidal desires. Identification with the father also gratifies the instinctual wish to share in the father's fantasied omnipotence by merging with him.

One of the most vital aspects of internalization is the development of the superego. Precursors to the superego occur in the vicissitudes of the weaning and toilet-training phases (Hartmann and Lowenstein, 1962). By identifying with the parents, the child resolves the conflict between his love for them and fear of castration in reprisal for sexual and aggressive wishes. In the identification process there is incorporation of the castration threat so that one experiences it from within.

The aggressive drive in normal development is fused with the libidinal and is modulated by the moderating influence of object love. This occurs as the child learns to perceive mother as both gratifier and frustrator. Aggression becomes bound or fused when there is a satisfying relationship to the love-object. Libidinal ties promote the availability of aggressive drive energies so they can be modified and subject to the dominant role of the ego. In addition to fusion, neutralization[1] and sublimation of aggressive drives divert their aims to more social goals; their energy then becomes available to the ego for its further development. The aggressive drive is the source of destructive behavior when something has gone wrong in childhood during the developmental phases.[2]

In the next phase of his theorizing, Freud explored more fully the area of "ego instincts." Nonlibidinal urges assumed an increasingly important role in his formulations.

---

[1] The capacity to neutralize aggression may be a criterion of ego strength. Internalization of nonneutralized aggression may embody a weak or eventually, masochistic ego (Hartmann *et al.*, 1949).

[2] Patterns of aggression depend on mental development and experience, vary from one stage of life to another, and seem "related to what hurts or frightens the child. A child's wish to kill or his fear of being killed often express a fantasy of genital mutilation and penetration rather than a primarily aggressive wish" (Brenner, 1971). Conflicts regarding separation-individuation; instances of parental deprivation, rejection, or schism; or considerations of sibling rivalry—rarely dealt with by Freud—also contribute to aggressive behavior.

He was no longer as concerned with the source of instincts as with their aims. The general goal of ego instincts emerged as self-preservation, the major constituent, aggression. Aggressive trends were transferred from aspects of libido, and incorporated into the ego instincts. Freud (1915b) believed aggressive urges could thus occur in the absence of sexual conflict:

> The ego hates, abhors and pursues with intent to destroy all objects which are for it a source of painful feelings, without taking into account whether they mean to it frustration of sexual satisfaction or gratification of the needs of self-preservation. Indeed it may be asserted that the true prototypes of the hate relation are derived not from sexual life but from the struggle of the ego for self-preservation and self-maintenance.

This revision of his earlier views emphasized the reactive nature of aggressive urges. Their source was not biological, as were sexual urges, but lay, rather, in the self-preservative tendency of the ego to retaliate or strike back in relation to threat or denial of satisfaction. This reactive view was adopted later by Dollard *et al.* (1939) who channeled it into behavioral terms in the frustration–aggression hypothesis, later modified by Miller *et al.* (1941) who felt frustration leads to variegated responses one of which may be aggression.

The destructiveness of World War I undoubtedly exerted a profound effect on Freud's theorizing. Subsequently he expanded his concept of aggression into his final, Thanatos theory (1920, 1923, 1930, 1940). *Civilization and Its Discontents* (1930) emphatically underlines Freud's conviction that "man is a wolf to man," that man can be a "savage beast to whom consideration towards his own kind is something alien." Since civilized society is perpetually threatened with disintegration . . . civilization has to use its utmost efforts to set limits to man's aggressive instincts . . . by psychical reaction formations. Hence, the use of methods intended to incite people into identifications and aim-inhibited relationships of love, hence the restriction upon sexual life, and hence too the ideal's commandment to love one's neighbor as oneself, [though] . . . nothing else runs so strongly counter to the original nature of man.

Modulating the aggressive instinct is the superego in the form of conscience. It inflicts the harshness or severity against the self that one originally wished to thrust upon others. Perhaps "the price we must pay for advances in civilization," theorized Freud, "is a loss of happiness through the heightening of the sense of guilt." In *Ego and the Id*, Freud pointed out that the sense of guilt approaches the pathological as one compares the cruelty of the superego with the sadistic traits of melancholia and obsessive neurosis. *Civilization and Its Discontents* stresses, however, the cultural attributes of the sense of guilt; the latter is now seen as the instrument culture uses not necessarily against libido but against one's aggressiveness. The sense of guilt is no longer viewed as merely the tension between ego and superego, but also as an "expression of the conflict due to ambivalence of the eternal struggle between Eros and the instinct of destruction or death."

Contemporary views regarding destructive aggression or sadism may be briefly mentioned: Lorenz (1966), in a theory similar to Freud's hypothesis in its results, indicates that man, like his animal ancestors, is motivated by a phylogenetically programmed, spontaneously flowing eruption of aggression, located in specific areas of the brain. If not properly channeled, this aggression accumulates and explodes.

The person seeks stimuli to help release the aggressive drive. However, the more this aggressive energy has accumulated, the less specific such a stimulus has to be, so that aggression may be triggered off even without an adequate stimulus.

According to Bieber (1966), sadism is a "defensive paranoid mechanism in which the victim is a personified representative of a variety of irrationally perceived threats; he must then be dominated, destroyed or injured." The sadistic personality evidences a composite of "rage, anxiety, relief, vengeance, and frenetic ecstasy," similar to feelings of triumph in defeating an irrationally perceived enemy or in eliminating a threat. Bieber feels both sexual and power systems are integrated in sexual sadism.

Storr (1968) believes that the enjoyment of another's pain is unique and pervasive in the human realm. He feels the reciprocal connection between dependency and aggression accountable for the aggressiveness of man. That is, man, compared to other species, is "peculiar" in the span of time elapsing from birth to maturity and hence in the length of time he remains dependent on others; therefore, the fantasy life of children is replete with aggressive reverberations enabling them to protect and assert their developing individuality.

Erich Fromm (1941; 1964; 1972) has written extensively on the roots of sadism and the related concepts of authoritarianism and destructiveness. Deeply interested in the questions of fascism and its nihilistic potential, he has inquired into the phenomena of international and civil wars, increasing use of torture, rising violence in the cities, and threat of nuclear war and has investigated sadism in this wider social context.

The essence of sadism, according to Fromm (1964), is the

drive for complete and absolute control over a living being . . . to make of him a helpless object of our will, to become his god, to do with him as one pleases. To humiliate him, to enslave him, are means toward this end, and the most radical aim is to make him suffer, since there is no greater power over another person than that of forcing him to undergo suffering without his being able to defend himself.

The most drastic form of sadistic control is torture and the infliction of physical pain. Less dramatic, though more pervasive, is the desire to humiliate, dominate, or make another individual part of oneself. Sadism is prompted by a sense of emotional impotency: The desire for power over another compensates for the incapacity to create or to love. The sadistic person needs to feel omnipotent so that another person becomes his "thing." The personality of Himmler, an obsessional, hoarding character with a need for absolute control, embodies the essence of sadism.

Still another sadistic tendency is the desire to exploit others, use them, steal from them, disembowel them, that is, incorporate anything "eatable" in them. This may subsume material things as well as the emotional or intellectual qualities of another individual. Often overlooked is the dependence of the sadistic person on the object of his sadism: His sense of strength devolves on his feeling of mastery over someone else.

Fromm suggests that both masochistic and sadistic trends are linked. He sees them as derivatives of that individual inability to tolerate isolation and personal inadequacy. This sets up a need for symbiosis—the merging of one individual self with another so that both are completely interdependent. The essential distinction between sadism and masochism is that in the first the destructiveness tends to be more conscious and directly transformed into action, while in the second the hostility is unconscious and indirect in its expression. Fromm also distinguishes between sadistic and destructive persons: The destructive person desires to annihilate the object, do away with and get rid of him; the sadistic individual wishes to dominate his object and therefore suffers loss himself should the object disappear. Perhaps the wish for power is the most important manifestation of sadism. With the rise of fascism and totalitarianism, the recognition of this craving for power has become more widespread as well as a conviction about its efficacy.

Destructiveness varies enormously among individuals and social groups. Fromm states that the lower middle classes in Europe, for example, have greater potential for destruction than the working or upper classes. Anthropological studies have also indicated that some cultures are inherently peaceful, cooperative, and nonexploitative, while others are hostile, treacherous, and paranoid. The quantity of destructiveness depends on the degree to which the "expansiveness of life is curtailed;" the "blockage of spontaneity of the growth and expression of man's sensuous, emotional and intellectual capacities" is minimized.

Fromm's most recent explorations of aggression suggest that today a significant source of aggression and destructiveness resides in the so-called bored character. This subjective state of boredom arises from the person's "inability to respond to things and people around him with real interest." The mode of compensation for this boredom is aggression to the point of violence[1] and destructiveness. Thus, the

---

[1] May (1972) finds that the appeal of violence has to do with "a uniting of the self in action." To those who never claimed a self, it is like a religious call. The "ecstasy of violence" is the only ecstasy of which such people are capable.

crucial motivation in the act of killing appears to be the desire to have the sensation of feeling alive or the excitement of making someone respond.

More extreme forms of these destructive trends are termed love of death or "necrophilia," "malignant narcissism," and "symbiotic incestuous fixation to mother," prompting one to destroy for the "sake of destruction" and to hate for the "sake of hate."

Fromm perceives the necrophilious person as a malignant extension of Freud's anal–sadistic character: "They are qualitatively alike in their interest in and affinity with the unalive and the dead." The necrophilious character is thus preoccupied with corpses, decay, feces, and dirt; ruminates about sickness, burials, or death; and is enamored of darkness and night. Hitler was obsessed with destruction, according to Fromm, and though at first it appeared he wished to destroy only those he considered enemies, he eventually cared only for "total and absolute destruction: that of the German people, of those around him and of himself." The necrophilious dwell in the past. They are cold, distant, and pursue a mechanical orderliness. For them, the fundamental polarity in life is between those having the power to kill and those who do not.

In viewing the death instinct as psychopathological, Fromm differs from Freud, who perceives it as a normal or universal phenomenon. In his discussion of "malignant narcissism," Fromm gives examples of megalomaniac leaders who "cured" their narcissism by transforming the world to fit their needs: From Caligula and Nero to Stalin and Hitler the need to annihilate all opponents, to "transform reality so that it fits their narcissism," is imperative.

The pathology of "incestuous fixation" prevents one from experiencing another as fully human; only those who share the same blood or soil are acknowledged.

Fusing extreme forms of necrophilia, narcissism, and incestuous symbiosis, Fromm proposes the entity "syndrome of decay," and again Hitler best personifies this: A person deeply attracted to death and destruction, narcissistic to the degree that the only reality for him lay in his own wishes and thoughts, and incestuous in his fanatical devotion to those who shared his blood tie.

Erikson (1950) suggests another view of Hitler. He indicates that "the father attributes" in Hitler's historical image are exaggerated. Hitler was "the Fuhrer: a glorified older brother" who wrested power from the fathers, avoiding any identification with them. Designating his father "old while still a child," he kept for himself the unique role of the one who remains young, in total control. He was the supreme adolescent, a gang leader who "kept the boys together" by his imperative need for admiration, producing terror and involving others in crimes from which there was no way back.

Also of interest is Erikson's discussion of Hitler's image of the "superhuman mothers." One discerns here a dual image: the mother on the one hand is playful, childlike, and generous; on the other hand, she is treacherous and identified with sinister forces. In Erikson's view, this is frequently noted in patriarchal societies where women in irresponsible and childlike roles become a "go-between and an in-between." Father "hates in her the elusive children and the children hate in her the aloof father." Since mother regularly becomes and remains the "unconscious model for the world," the ambivalence toward the maternal woman became a central feature of German official thinking. Hitler saw himself as a lonely man struggling and ingratiating himself with superhuman mother figures, who were seeking to both annihilate and "bless" him.

Perhaps we can further elaborate on the nuances of

sadism by returning to the Marquis de Sade, from whose name and ideas the term sadism as a psychological entity was originally extracted. One might say his personality and writings though complex, in part give expression to human malignance in an extreme and exaggerated form, despite the glossing over of his aberrations by writers who extol the man as an upsetter of convention (Wilson, 1965) or champion his ideas as an exuberant expression of individuality or as an affirmation of self (de Beauvoir, 1953b). In his writings de Sade stands for annihilation and world destruction and repeatedly states his desire to eliminate the human race and to pulverize the universe totally. In *Justine* (1791) he presents a misanthropic chemist who has devised a method for creating artificial eruptions that will devastate cities: "He will watch from a mountain and will not have to depend on another human being for indulging his lust." In this way the final interest linking the chemist to other people will be repudiated. Hitler, who presided over the holocaust of World War II, embodied something of de Sade's insane chemist—his mad exhilaration in power and his contempt for human life.

Bach and Schwartz (1972) help to clarify the murkiness, confusion, romanticization, and censure surrounding the Marquis de Sade in their psychoanalytic exploration of a dream and a group of perverse fantasies from his prison writings, *The 120 Days of Sodom* (1785). They view the latter as an effort to deal with problems of narcissistic decompensation and suggest that the public image of de Sade comprises a "delusional grandiose self" in line with Kohut's (1971) concept of narcissistic pathology. This "delusional identity" is repeatedly promulgated in extended variations and permutations as noted in de Sade's relentless desire to restore a "grandiose self representation," traumatically interfered with in childhood. That is, in childhood, de

Sade was persuaded by his parents, for presumably opportunistic purposes, to play with the young prince Louis de Bourbon,[1] close to him in age. After a violent quarrel with the boy, de Sade was sent to live with his grandmother, and his parents simultaneously went abroad. De Sade was unable to assimilate the narcissistic insult of having to view himself as inferior or secondary to his playmate. His temper tantrum represents his violent antipathy toward the prince who threatened de Sade's quest for power and interfered with the relationship with his mother, regarding whom there remained a pervasive sense of separation and loss, as particularly evidenced in his writings. The episode may also be seen as a screen memory for "traumatic disillusionment" with self and parents, eventuating in an enhancement of his imperious, grandiose pretensions.

Bach and Schwartz maintain that de Sade suffered from a formal thought disorder leading to suicidally depressive and paranoid trends. His grandiose and megalomaniacal states helped him endure his protracted incarceration. The authors indicate that de Sade's prison writings are decisive in his attempts to preserve some measure of restitutive identity.

Prior to his imprisonment de Sade participated in perverse, sadomasochistic practices. His writings perpetuate his acting out, serving the dual purpose of eliciting punishment and, in addition, serving as a crucial determinant towards his self-affirmation. Fantasies of revenge also serve the function of affirmation and are aimed at his persecutors as well,

---

[1] De Sade's mother, lady-in-waiting at the palace to the Princess de Condé, was involved in rearing the young prince on the death of the prince's parents, about a year after the birth of the Marquis. Presumably his mother was supposed to name the Marquis, Louis, but he was mistakenly named François. De Sade never accepted the mistake and continued to call himself Louis.

though one discerns underneath them, a fantasy that the person who negated his grandiose self-image must be repeatedly annihilated. De Sade identifies with the aggressor who "ravishes, despoils and murders a beautiful and innocent child, a representative of the perfect childhood self." Here sadistic fantasies postpone the final fragmentation of the delusional self, warding off submission, which is equated with death.

Masochistic fantasies emerge as extreme attempts to restitute delusionally idealized images. The perversions in *The 120 Days of Sodom* shift from masochism to sadism and eventually to murder as the idealized images are extinguished. The authors view the masochistic fantasies as

> restitutional attempts to reanimate and cling to idealized imagos which have been denied and destroyed as their promised omnipotence failed . . . followed by a return to more archaic fantasies of the delusional self whose existence is validated and affirmed through sadism and murder.

It is the narcissistic fantasy "a child is being murdered"—that is, his childhood grandiose self is annihilated or abandoned—repeatedly reenacted and denied, that finds central expression in the murderous, sadistic fantasies of *The 120 Days of Sodom*. In addition to the need for survival of the delusional self, there is considerable intrapsychic conflict between this survival and the wish to die.

Schafer (1954), in his description of the Rorschach records of sadistic personalities, emphasizes qualities of hostility, attack, violence, or destructiveness in his subjects or points to an authoritarian orientation having to do with implications of power and subjugation of others.

In my records of masochistic personalities, however, aggression or rebelliousness rarely appear as conscious or externalized. Rather, central themes here have to do with feelings of being oppressed, burdened, or deprived. Human figures are projected as "kneeling" or "begging." There is a sense of mutilation, of "something being pulled apart...," of the "blood of virginity—repulsive." Feelings of being damaged or ruined are frequent. There is a concern with aging and death and a marked oral dependency manifested in "mouths open," "breast," "food." Such comments as "something very threatening about this, vampire or ghost, someone about to attack or envelop or close in on you, menacing" convey anxiety about being punished, engulfed, or overwhelmed. Feelings of rejection, too, are present: "Figure turned around, going away from you." There is a lack of clear-cut perception of self, a somewhat tentative attitude toward the adult role, and the assumption of a weak, helpless position. A dysphoric mood is expressed in: "mask of tragedy," "sad cow."

Instances of a more aggressive approach are evidenced in responses such as "two dragons spouting fire" or "cannibals cooking;" or aggression is modulated, as in "smiling lion." In the main, however, patients described in this study cling to feelings of victimization or resort to self-inflating dreams or fantasies, sometimes replete with vengeful retaliation, but more often dealing with self-injury or self-debasement. Anger is deflected in psychosomatic symptoms or in defense mechanisms, such as denial, reaction formation, projection or introjection.

Identification with the aggressor—with the original parental figure who is rejecting—is considered by some the most powerful mechanism in the masochist's armamentarium. Here the individual feels he is doing the "right thing," pleasing the sadistic partner whose love he craves, and, in addition, hopes to gain approval by emulating the aggressive trends of the partner even to the point of losing his own identity (Berliner, 1958). In my patients this mechanism emerged only in fantasy. Nydes (1963) pointed to identification with the aggressor in his elaboration of the sadistic orientation. When present, the aggressive, vindictive or provocative attitudes of the masochist, the drive to punish through failure and unhappiness, are secondary to his "bid for the affection of a hating object . . ." (Berliner, 1958).

Brenman (1952) suggests that projective attitudes, when present in a masochistic framework, may be used as a vehicle for:

> a benevolent paranoid attitude, where the usual denials of and reaction formations against hostile impulses are projected wholesale, and people are seen as essentially good and without malice, the Polly-annaism so familiar in the masochist.

In examining the literature on masochism, one notes two distinct tendencies. Some view the masochist predominantly as an intensely suffering person, victimized by the cruelties of his environment. Others see him as blackmailing, coercive, or paranoid, as someone who, through suffering, is excused from taking part in life and usually manipulates others into taking care of him. One might, therefore, postulate a continuum of masochistic attitudes ranging from the muted, placating, completely acquiescent, passive, enslaved individual to the demanding, contentious, complaining person, armed for a power struggle. The masochistic character, unlike the sadistic, is, for the most part, completely unaware of his provocativeness. The sadistic personality possesses a weak, impotent, or crippled sense of self but is intent on self-aggrandizement and the acquisition of force. He lives aggressively and destructively through others and needs to enslave, humiliate, destroy, or exploit his partner. Perhaps there is some degree of vindictive triumph in the conviction that others may be as degraded or afflicted as he unconsciously feels himself to be.

Thus, it appears that the manner in which masochism and sadism are intertwined has to do not so much with "reversal into the opposite" or "turning round upon the subject's own self" as with interacting reciprocities where the underlying characterological patterns and motivation differ for each partner.

VIII. The Pleasure in Pain

What is meant by the "joy" of suffering, the merging of pain and pleasure?

Freud's pleasure–pain concept of behavior initially appeared in *The Interpretation of Dreams* (1900), to be followed by "Formulations Regarding the Two Principles in Mental Functioning" (1911). In elaborating his "pleasure principle," designated as "a special case of Fechner's tendency to stability," Freud pointed to the "sovereign tendency" of primary or unconscious processes that "strive toward gaining pleasure," avoiding situations that "arouse unpleasantness or pain." At first Freud defined pleasure and pain in regard to the quantity of excitation or tension present: "There is an attempt on the part of the psychic apparatus to keep the quantity of excitation as low as possible, or at least constant." To accelerate the quantity of excitation is felt as painful, contrary to function. Pain is experienced as increased tension, pleasure as decreasing tension. Presumably, in Freud's system, excitement is noxious, and neutral affects are optimally desirable.

The psysiological basis of masochistic phenomena, which Freud considered an intermingling of pain and pleasure, was assumed to be the tendency of infants to respond to "any increase in psychic tension with sexual excitement." Thus, according to Freud, painful tensions could lead to sexual responses in infancy. The linking of pain with sexual excitement in infancy was "burnt up" in later life, though it remained as a physiological substrate, eventually layered by the psychic superstructure to form erogenous masochism.[1] Freud felt this predilection is more intense[2] for some individuals than others and provides the basis for the sexual excitement experienced by masochistic

---

[1] Greenacre (1952) felt that sexual overstimulation and, in particular, premature genital stimulation of the child arouses anxiety and leads to an overflow from the stimulated area to other erotogenic zones, resulting in diffused discharge processes with corresponding affective experiences that blend pleasurable and directly painful sensual and feeling qualities. Nacht and Racamier (1960) introduce a similar concept: Before the "subject–object" distinction is solidly established, the tensions produced by frustration are neither externalized nor channeled into any structured defensive circuit; thus the energy that will later emerge in aggression is neither "repressed nor inflected but penetrates and spreads into and impregnates the whole organism," establishing a "primitive organic masochism."

[2] All affects, even those that are unpleasant, are capable of eliciting pleasure upon attaining a unique or particular intensity. Beyond certain limits, however, these affects might become painful. Determining the threshold, as well as the nature of the painful sensations capable of eliciting pleasure, is variable for each person in Freud's view.

perverts in situations where bodily pain is inflicted by themselves or a partner. The instinctual basis for masochism is Thanatos, the death urge. Fusion of self-directed destructiveness and self-directed libido accounts for the pleasure in pain. Freud speculated that a self-oriented destructive drive exists from birth, functioning concurrently and in conflict with the pleasure principle.

Hartmann *et al.* (1949) point out that pure aggressive release can induce pleasure. Though the primary goal of aggression is not the pursuit of pleasure, sheer aggressive forces are normally mobilized and required in situations of danger in the service of self-preservation and need not be envisaged as a struggle between death and life instincts.

Though Freud in "The Economic Problem in Masochism" (1924) wrote that pleasurable tension and "painful" lowering of tension could occur and that pleasure and pain could thus depend more on some peculiarly qualitative factor regarding stimulus tension, he did not revise his concept of pleasure to accommodate this insight. Subsequently, due to the need for self-preservation, the pleasure principle is replaced by the reality principle, which,

> without abandoning the ultimate attainment of pleasure, yet demands and enforces the postponement of satisfaction, the renunciation of manifold possibilities of it, and the temporary endurance of "pain" on the long and circuitous road to pleasure.

Civilization and Its Discontents (1928) reiterated that the pleasure principle

> dominates the operation of the mental apparatus from the very beginning; there can be no doubt about its efficiency and yet its program is in conflict with the whole world. The intention that men should be "happy" is not

included in the scheme of "Creation." What is called happiness . . . comes from the satisfaction of pent-up needs that have reached great intensity and by its very nature can only be a transitory experience.

Happiness consists in the avoidance of pain and unpleasure, in the sudden satisfaction of highly pent-up need tensions. There is an identification of happiness with pleasure in embodying the sudden decrease of the accumulated excitation of need tension.

In *Outline of Psychoanalysis* (1940) Freud continues along similar lines:

The ego's activities are governed by considerations of the tensions produced by stimuli present within it or introduced into it. The raising of these tensions is in general felt as unpleasure and their lowering as pleasure. It is probable however that what is felt as pleasure or unpleasure is not the absolute degree of the tensions but something in the rhythm of their changes. The ego pursues pleasure and seeks to avoid unpleasure. The consideration that the pleasure principle requires a reduction or perhaps ultimately the extinction of the tension of the instinctual needs, that is, a state of Nirvana, leads to problems still unexamined in the relations between the pleasure principle and the two primal forces, Eros and the death instinct.

Others in the Freudian fold have written on the constellation of pain and pleasure. Alexander (1924) indicates that the child, in noting that its forbidden deeds are eradicated by the punishment that follows, learns to seek out its punishment "gladly" in order to be absolved from the sins committed.

Reich (1933) has also clarified the presumed "pleasure

in pain" experience: In his view, the masochist strives for pleasure, although frustration, anxiety, and fear of punishment interfere, so that the original goal is obliterated and "made unpleasant." Though it might appear as if the masochist is seeking "unpleasure," actually "anxiety comes between." The desired pleasure is then perceived as the anticipated danger and "end-pleasure is replaced by end-unpleasure." For Reich, a repetition compulsion beyond the pleasure principle is not warranted. According to him, masochistic phenomena can best be explained within the framework of the pleasure principle and fear of punishment.

Further elucidating the nature of "pleasure in pain" Reik (1941) suggests that by anticipating the dreaded punishment, instinctual enjoyment may eventuate. The masochistic scene or fantasy has a dual nature: first the discomfort, humiliation, or punishment; then pleasure and instinctual gratification. First the atonement, then the sin.

Fenichel (1945) points to the paradox that a feared pain might be avoided or denied by suffering pain. This occurs when certain experiences may have so firmly fixated sexual pleasure in connection with pain that suffering becomes necessary. It is not originally, but secondarily sought as the price to be paid to avoid disturbing guilt feelings. Masochistic activities follow the mechanism of "sacrifice," indicating that the price paid beforehand is supposed to appease the gods.

The combination of severe frustrations and prohibitions with premature sexual overstimulation "will tend to fixate and internalize anxious and painful affective discharge and to fuse it with pleasurable modes of affective discharge," resulting in masochistic behavior (Jacobson, 1953). Masochistic perversions point to "an extreme pathological example of fusions between unpleasurable and pleasurable affect components." With regard to moral masochistic formations and depressive affective states, the pleasure principle may become a victim of "economic necessities." In describing depression and suicide, Jacobson asserts the aggressive drives are not necessarily "beyond the pleasure principle," nor do they aim at the total elimination of tension. Rather the pleasure principle seeks to reestablish psychic equilibrium by restoring the homeostatic principle. Ultimately, in thus striving to lower the high tension level at any cost, the homeostatic principle does not succeed in its aim of self-preservation. It can only accomplish a total removal of tension via self-destruction.

The pleasure principle supersedes the homeostatic principle in manic states, however; here aggressive energy is repeatedly mobilized and discharged, effecting a distortedly pleasurable emotional condition. Despite the primacy of the pleasure principle in this condition, it may deteriorate "to the point of a general energetic impoverishment" quite as dangerous as the suicidal pattern.

Since restrictive parents defeat the child's defiant rage, his pursuit of forbidden pleasure may take the form of "pain-dependency." This is defined by Rado (1959) as the forced and mechanical pursuit of pain or "advance punishment"—the only means by which the child can feel free to fulfill his forbidden desires. Here the anticipation of pleasure overrules the deterrent action of pain. Through this expectation, punishment becomes a paradoxical stimulus for pleasure, enhanced in its value by the "aesthetic effect of contrast."

A "seeking of pleasure in unpleasure," without any implication of self-injury or guilt feeling, may occur in children's play, as Lowenstein (1957) points out in his discussion of an 11-month-old girl playfully reprimanded by her grandmother for sucking her thumb. During the game the baby apprehensively observed the stern face of her grandmother. As her grandmother began to smile, however, the child laughed and proceeded to suck her thumb once again. If grandmother remained unsmiling, the child began to cry. She sought to have the adult smile or show that "affectionate complicity which undoes the prohibition and eliminates the danger of not being loved."

In playful exchanges between adults and children punitive threats as well as their "pleasurable removal" often synchronize. Children frequently request innumerable repetitions of such activities. This mode of behavior, pervasive in childhood play, could be a precursor to future masochistic behavior, in its seeking out of conditions involving danger, fear, and unpleasure, as well as their modulation through collusion with the punitive parent. The pleasure is initially not dependent upon the pain itself but on its removal through reunion with the parent. The pain emanating from the threat, and the pleasure over its removal, apparently become intertwined. The child's apprehension in being thrown into the air, losing his equilibrium, or being threatened with pain or hurt may well become pleasurable should the parents participate with "loving complicity." The readiness with which some children switch from anticipating removal of a threat to anticipating a threat may point to the burgeoning of a future tendency to seek out masochistic situations. Constitutional predispositions regarding this modality may be reinforced via excessive stimulation. From the vantage point of survival, these pregenital mechanisms assist the child—whose role is helpless or dependent—in coping with frustrations and threats coming from the parent.

Lowenstein also describes mixed "autoaggressive and autoerotic" activities in which pain might be intermingled with pleasure. In some cases, pain is present first, as, for example, in the irritation of itching or the sensations produced by swelling of the mucosae of the gums. These, in turn, cause reflex responses, simultaneously pain relieving, painful, and pleasurable, such as scratching, clamping the jaws, teeth-grinding, and biting.

In his restructuring of the more traditional concepts of pain and pleasure, Szasz (1957) places them in the context of biological factors on the one hand, and object relationships and communication processes, on the other. He debunks the notion that pleasure consists simply in the absence of pain or that it is principally the satisfaction of a pressing bodily need. In psychoanalysis, he continues, the concept of pleasure is regarded as an affect both stemming from and reflecting physiological processes. There is a predilection for linking all pleasure to a sexual frame of reference related to bodily functions, whether oral, anal, or genital. Interpersonal relationships and social behavior are labeled as pleasure producing, either in leading to bodily gratification or via "sublimation." The pleasure inherent in sublimated behavior is perceived as less intense, "as if these intensities were measurable and comparable," than the satisfactions of "presumably unaltered erotic needs." Szasz contrasts Freud's theory of pleasure with one encompassing the tenets of ego psychology. The latter views pleasure as a signal or affect experienced by the ego whenever a past, traumatic situation is mastered. It further indicates that lack of mastery or competence is linked with anxiety or unpleasure, achievement with pleasure.

Szasz presents a many-leveled orientation regarding the varied meanings of pleasure. The primary model of pleasure involves a process of physiological need reduction, a signal of safety indicating a satisfactory relationship between ego and body. Since in this early period the ego predominantly alerts one to danger, it will experience painful affects more frequently than those that are pleasurable.

The next level in the "hierarchical" development of the concept of pleasure has to do with the awareness of human objects:

An intimate linkage between bodily need satisfaction and certain types of object relationships is established in the early months. . . . What is significant for the conception of pleasure is that by virtue of such linkages the experience of pleasure becomes immensely enlarged from its previous meaning. Certain types of human relationships henceforth will also be experienced as pleasurable.

In this sense pleasure is viewed as a communication concept involving two persons and may be contrasted with the communicative meaning of pain, which variously expresses accusation directed at a significant person, a command to action, a request for help, complaint at being unfairly treated, or an attack against a needed but unconsciously hated object. Pleasure calls for no action. Rather, it indicates that a relationship has been good or satisfying, perhaps suggesting a perpetuation of the status quo.[1]

---

[1] Jacobson (1953) assumes that, despite our desire to avoid pain and achieve pleasure, we may not necessarily wish this pleasurable experience to go on forever. There is a need for variability "either for higher pleasure or a different pleasure quality. The urge for a change during the sexual forepleasure phase would not appear to express the wish for relief but the wish for a climax;" in the orgastic excitement there is the hope for final "relief pleasure." Finally, "in a situation of relief after a period of enjoyable relaxation, we can observe an increasing need for stimuli inducing a different type—an excitement pleasure." To summarize, "tension pleasure may induce the urge for higher excitement; climactic pleasure, the urge for relief; and relief pleasure, the longing again for pleasurable tension." Such a schema reflects the dynamic changes in the patterns of pleasure and unpleasure deriving from the demands of reality. In particular, pleasure alternates "between excitement and relief pleasures which correspond to rises and falls of psychic excitation around a medium level."

Szasz suggests that in the course of maturation pain, anxiety, mourning, and a sense of shame or guilt may be associated with separation, bodily injury, or loss of mastery, whereas pleasure is associated with "gain" or "something being added," as in relief from hunger, sexual satisfaction, contentment, happiness, religious absorption, and so on. Insofar as the expectation of the gain is directed toward a human object who must supply the want, this additive notion of pleasure includes the implication of an object relationship. It is preferable, continues Szasz, to view the nature of human development not as a shift necessitating the gradual abandonment of pleasure as a goal and its substitution by "painful reality" but rather as a process of transformation that inevitably includes changes in the very concept of "pleasure" and "pain." To regard all pleasure as fundamentally a matter of need reduction is to force all later symbolic complexities back into the framework of its earliest conceptual prototype.

Schachtel's (1959) views on pleasure are also of interest. He questions a pleasure concept based on the desire to return to a state without stimulation, excitation, or striving,[1] as well as the assumption that only acknowledgment of the reality principle and the longing to retain or acquire the love of one's parents prompts the child to give up his wish to return to a tensionless state. He suggests, furthermore, that Freud originally defined the affect of pleasure as the "unpleasure" principle because of the negative implication of relief from excitation. In this sense Freud's pleasure concept might be identical with the death instinct, the wish to return

---

[1] The infantile intolerance of tension is also an expression of the child's inability to discharge through the channels of mature ego functions, sublimations, and adult instinctual activity. The child cannot bear tension, for whose adequate and pleasurable affective and motor discharge his psychic organization is not yet equipped.

to a state of complete quiescence, a state of inorganic matter. Life is seen in the context of pain, disturbance, and want, death as relief from these. The pleasure principle joins with the death instinct in seeking to abolish the painful stimulation of life. Freud has described pleasure not as such but in the state of "embeddedness,"[1] in relief from pain, irritation and tension. Though Freud evidenced a more realistic view of the child than his predecessors, he ironically enough shared his culture's negative attitudes towards his own discoveries. He perceived the child as "polymorphously perverse," propelled by "drives striving for discharge in passive satisfaction or in violent affect storms, a creature whose development depended entirely on the control, taming or suppression of those drives and affects." Freud depicted affects as hysterical attacks generated by past traumatic experiences, elicited in situations similar to those in which they originally occurred, neglecting the positive communication function of affects and counterposing affects to action.

Schachtel offers an alternative conception of pleasure and affect. A pleasure concept based on relief from excitation is seen as inconsistent with the tremendous surplus energy found in young children. It may be applied to early infancy, old age, early stages of convalescence after an illness, or the return to sleep—states defined by a "weakened or immature condition of the organism or its need for rest." But "childhood, youth, maturity, awakedness are characterized by heightened aliveness, intensity of interest, zest for

---

[1] By "embeddedness" Schachtel refers to a mode of existence "completely sheltering and nourishing," from which the organism directly obtains its energy supply without having to go after it. "Since the organism's needs would be continuously supplied there would be no need tensions." In such a situation Freud's pleasure principle would be valid.

living." One can define pleasure as the desire for and enjoyment of stimulation and activity, rather than the wish to get rid of them. At different periods of life or of a particular day there is a continuum of behavior ranging from sheer relief of tension to the eager anticipation of stimulation and enjoyment of activity. Overlooked by Freud was the infant's propensity for active searching, satisfaction, discovery, and exploration plus the fact the child enjoys these capacities and does not see stimulation as an intrusion. These early predilections—the child's pleasure and fulfillment in the encounter with an expanding reality and in the exercise of his growing capacities and skills—may, of course, be submerged in obeisant yielding to cultural imperatives and the conventionalization imposed by parents, teachers, or peers.

To some extent Freud's view of sexual pleasure as the sudden discharge in orgasm of pent-up need tension, Schachtel suggests, led to his negative concept of pleasure as cessation of excitation. Actually, sexual pleasure is complexly intertwined with other emotions, such as affection, love, anger, power, need for recognition, or need for nurturance. These emotions are central, whether sexual pleasure has to do with relief from tension or is embodied in the positive pleasure of relatedness to another. Freud minimized the pleasurable character of sexual excitement, terming this mere forepleasure as contrasted with the orgastic end-pleasure viewed entirely as discharge gratification. Though he questioned this explanation later on, he failed to revise his theory of sexual pleasure.

To return to masochistic phenomena, these deal not so much with pleasure in pain, as with helpless or inexorable repetition of situations involving feelings of defeat and humiliation. These latter emanate from an undermining or unaffirming interpersonal exchange, set up by the mother figure in the oral phase and reinforced in later development by pathological family interactions. The individual's crippled self-image continues to accommodate the frustrating or depriving parent (or surrogate) by failure and suffering. Though often provocative or retaliative, these latter attitudes are secondary to underlying and more basic feelings of powerlessness and weakness and serve to perpetuate the lethal interactions.

Where masochistic suffering seems to be "enjoyed" or to give pleasure, one must question the subjective meaning, as well as cultural context of such "pleasure." The subjective feeling of being "happy," when not a quality of the state of well being of the entire person, is illusory. What might be meant is need for drama, crisis, sensation, stimulation, or a high tension level, thereby emphasizing one's identity or acquiring a spurious feeling of aliveness.

Genuine or autonomous feelings are, for the most part, deadened or muted in masochistic persons. Life is generally experienced as occurring outside their orbit, as not to be responded to but to be reacted to in submission, at times to the point of self-extinction. The center of gravity is found outside themselves or is "centrifugally directed" (Kelman, 1959). To comprehend the puzzling situation where suffering may involve satisfaction, one must note that other modes of satisfaction are closed to masochistic personalities. Self-assertive or constructive activities are avoided, and should they be attempted, they are accompanied by such excessive anxiety as to obviate any pleasure to be gained. In addition, because of the need for dependency or unobtrusiveness there is little gratification to be derived from recognition or success. Satisfactions are therefore greatly restricted and attainable only through some route of safety.

In my patients an oppositional dualism with another helps maintain the needed high-tension state. A destructive relationship may frequently be more tolerable than one that is positive. An overwhelming number of patients, predominantly female, require sadomasochistic fantasies involving rape or other self-debasing experiences to feel optimally sexually aroused. For example, B. projects fantasies of sexual intercourse where the male urinates on the woman, or two men are "in her front and back," setting up feelings of victimization and ensuing vengeful, retaliatory attitudes. W. complains that her husband is not a great painter or that he is obese and has a monotonous voice. Or she corrects his grammar, completes his sentences, or compares his I.Q. unfavorably with hers. Occasionally, when they are making love, she sings old camp songs. She is glad she can "turn off" her sexual feelings. Then she isn't under anyone's control. Sex is experienced as humiliating, a bargaining situation. She can only become aroused via masochistic fantasies of being bound, raped, and then having group intercourse. Her husband cannot give her the abuse she needs. W. reproaches him because he has not given her anything she can "live through." She feels she does not possess a "real self." She thrives on her anger and obtains a false sense of aliveness in this way. At first she didn't like me because she felt she couldn't provoke me. To her, I seemed overly relaxed and undefensive. Her husband, she feels, does not vitalize her enough or give her sufficient sensation, stimulation, or pain, as did her mother.

In actuality, the masochistic person "enjoys" suffering as little as others do. As regards the so-called tendency of painful stimuli to enhance sexual response, Bieber (1966) indicates that anxiety itself may set off and reinforce sexual excitation. He states that, physiologically, anxiety and sexual arousal are excitatory reactions and, furthermore, that masochism is always accompanied by anxiety, since all masochistic behavior—sexual and nonsexual—is aimed at self-injury.

The "pleasure in pain" orientation may find some degree of validation in the stress in modern American and Western-European culture on the value of pain and suffering as a necessary prelude to salvation. This indicates, both to the superego and to others, that we are good or striving to be good. Pain and suffering might be all too readily substituted for goal-directed effort and accomplishment. Thus, the "romantic" notion that pain, suffering, or anguish are necessary ingredients for creativity and artistic achievement.

Of considerable interest are those personalities with intact ego strength, who, for rational purposes, embrace situations involving pain, danger, or uncertainty—for example, revolutionary or social causes—and experience satisfaction in doing so. Or there are "task-oriented" personalities who enjoy absorption in an activity for its own sake or deem pleasurable what others may consider burdensome or hard work.

IX. Psychotherapy and Masochism

Freud (1937) in discussing the concept of "negative therapeutic reaction," the resistances encountered in analysis and the clinging to illness and suffering, suggested that the basis for this lies in the pervasiveness of guilt feelings and need for punishment. Viewing the "whole picture made up of the phenomena of the masochism inherent in so many people, of the negative therapeutic reaction and of the neurotic's sense of guilt"—with particular reference to the occasional exaggeration of symptoms following a correct interpretation, instead of the modulation as one might expect—Freud reiterated the inadequacy of the pleasure principle and reaffirmed the inexorableness of the death instinct. He questioned the efficacy of working with masochistic character traits, though he felt more optimistic whenever the etiology involved identification with a masochistic parent, "an incorporated rather than a genuine masochism."

Concerning masochistic transference formations, Freud (1922) noted, in comparing psychoanalysis and hypnosis, that inasmuch as the hypnotist evokes a "passive masochistic attitude" in the patient, similar to the relationship with father, and since there is some degree of suggestion in both hypnosis and analysis, masochistic attitudes may similarly be elicited in the transference manifestations of the analytic patient.

According to Menaker (1942) masochistic attitudes in analysis are attributable not only to transference phenomena but also to the inherent relationship of analyst and patient in the therapeutic milieu:

The mere fact that the analyst has the upper hand in the sense of understanding the patient, making interpretations, being responsible for the further progress of the analysis and, within limits, for its therapeutic outcome, makes it unavoidable that his ego dominates the patient's ego and provides an excellent opportunity for a repetition of the childhood wish for dependence and submission.

Other ingredients contributing to the analyst's dominance or authoritativeness and to a parent–child constellation are the prone position on the couch, the fact that the analyst arranges time and place, asks for free associations, verbally communicates or is silent, or offers interpretations. Both analyst and parent represent authorities in relation to whom patient and child must conform for therapy to succeed and for the child to be socialized. Both engender some degree of narcissistic hurt, since the child's ego thereby learns the limitations of its omnipotence.

The analyst should assume a fairly "human role," continues Menaker and avoid an "omnipotent role," minimizing the possibility of masochistic formations and affording the patient's ego "emotional sustenance." Perhaps the analyst's warmth and friendliness can gratify and strengthen the ego of the patient, modulating the circuit of sadomasochistic interactions and helping him avoid overly extreme masochistic reaction patterns.

In another paper, Menaker (1953) warns that in order to avert a masochistic reaction, the analyst must refrain from establishing a symbiosis with his patient in the transference situation. The patient she was referring to tended to "act-out" her neurotic character traits, which proved desirable since so much libido was placed in personal relationships that little remained for the transference. Such patients are like children. The "precipitates of the processes of identification" are still undeveloped; the ego is minimally formed and problems are "acted out as in the child's life rather than as fantasies in the transference."

Also decisive in deflecting a masochistic reaction in the transference situation was Menaker's attempt to structure the analytic setting as one in which the patient does not become obeisant to an overidealized, exalted parent-image. Menaker's patient gave tribute to this unique (for her) aspect of her relationship to the analyst: "You are the first and only adult toward whom I feel equal." For the first time she did not view herself as a child vulnerable to the world of adults. Menaker indicates that via her respectfulness of the patient's needs, in addition to "an avoidance of any hint of authoritarianism in the analytic procedure, an expressed belief in her potentialities for growth as an independent person, a genuine sympathy for her plight, a conscious presentation of myself as human and fallible," she was able to inculcate an atmosphere of equality, making possible "a new type of identification with the analyst."

Concurring with this stance, Berliner (1958) affirms that unlike those who are convinced of the need to be cold and distant concerning the masochistic patient in order to elicit the presumed sadistic trends, he prefers an emotional climate where the patient perhaps for the first time in his life, encounters a human being who offers "friendly understanding." Thus the analyst eliminates the criticism, punishment, or "libidinized suffering" so habitual to the masochistic patient. Berliner's therapeutic goals with such patients lie primarily in making explicit that the patient's need for the love of the rejecting partner results in an acceptance of suffering "as though it were love." Secondly, he seeks to help the patient perceive that this need to punish the love-object perpetuates his suffering. Finally, he hopes to demonstrate that the patient's hostility "is not his own" but stems from the parents' actual hostility towards him in infancy and childhood.

The masochisic patient is viewed by Berliner as the product of a traumatic childhood, as well as a "troublemaker" entangling himself in actual conflicts where he repeatedly emerges as a victim. Berliner focuses on analyzing the victim rather than the troublemaker. Like Menaker he also seeks to avoid the development of an intense transference to the therapist by giving priority to the transference aspects of other relationships.

Guilt feelings are analyzed by pointing to their component parts. For Berliner, these are the "need for affection" and the "experience of the punishing parent," which may eliminate moralistic implications. Actually, Berliner suggests, the "sense of defeat" is substituted for sense of guilt: "It is the defeat by a rejecting parent or parent substitute in transference; and it is this defeat rather than guilt that is introjected and forms a character pattern for acting out." By placing responsibility on the punitive parent rather than the instinctual processes in the child, there is minimal acting-out in the analysis itself.

Furthermore, the processes of "identification with the aggressor" permeate the phase of working through:

> All the features of the illness are recapitulated in the analysis of the identification. This work often stimulates the interest and cooperation of the patient. The patient learns to differentiate between love and hate and to adjust his life accordingly.

Suicidal or psychosomatic complications may emerge should the patient be involved in unrewarding life situations. The recognition late in life that there are hostilities in others of which the patient was not aware because of his defensive structure may result in temporary depression or paranoid behavior. One must be alerted to self-destructive tendencies in individuals who act out preoedipal libidinal needs concomitant to deep and intense association with frustration.

Kelman (1959), in exploring the heightened state of tension so central in and necessary to masochistic patients—and which he feels frequently becomes a numbing narcotic—suggests that should their tension level diminish for some reason, masochistic patients might panic in ultimately experiencing what was originally warded off. Their contact with reality may lessen, their sense of identity recede. Feelings of uncontrolled anxiety, thoughts of dissolution, suicidal self-hate, or a psychotic episode may ensue.

The only possibility of successful therapy with masochistic patients in Thompson's (1959) view is in dealing with their suffering as hostile aggression, after giving recognition, however, to the real cruelties described by the patient.

Though these may be genuine enough, the patient must learn to perceive his own contribution in creating the situation. Should the analyst be susceptible to the patient's appeal for rescue from the persecutor, the analyst is then accused by the patient of creating undue pressure. That is, should the patient obtain the analyst's sympathetic involvement, he seeks to frustrate it, so loath is he to break up the sadomasochistic relationship. Possibly in these situations a "hate relationship is more bearable than loneliness, and there is no hope of achieving a love relationship." The two factors severely impeding therapy are the enormous degree of attention obtained via suffering, which, by the nature of its excessive demands, antagonizes the sympathizer or provokes rejection, and the masochist's skill in turning the analyst's attention to the persecutor.

Bieber (1966) finds that patients with masochistic trends are problematic in terms of therapeutic success. Patients who spend all their time repeating countless injustices inflicted upon them are "acting out masochistically" as well as defeating treatment. The primary therapeutic task is to clarify unrealistic beliefs associated with irrational premises regarding anticipated injury. Should punishment and injury cease being linked with gratification, sexual or otherwise, the patient may begin to think more critically concerning his self-destructive defenses.

Also in contradistinction to the classical role, which functions chiefly by interpretation of the unconscious leading to masochistic transference to the analyst, Eisenbud (1967) strives for an atmosphere aimed at "restoring confidence, perceiving unused resources, revealing unperceived choices, and proving love is available and allowable." She notes, however, that the patient will employ therapy as a "courtroom," reinforcing his conviction that his partner is the aggressor and he, the victim. Though there are breakthroughs in life and analysis, the patient may still cling to the secondary gains. However, change may occur via the emergence of the "hidden introject of the sadist" whereby the patient seeks to manipulate another. The analyst's stress here on secondary gain and the patient's own sadism may reinforce the transference, i.e., patient as victim of the analyst. Eisenbud is convinced that should the analyst permit the patient to "win," the masochistic trends may be modulated.

Eidelberg (1959) finds that the problem of recognizing and resolving infantile omnipotence is crucial in treating masochistic patients. Therefore, it is necessary, as these emerge in the transference, to work with the patient's fantasies of omnipotence, noted in his power to evoke failure and punishment as evidence of a magical control of the environment. Following this, the analyst must convey to the patient that cessation of masochistic behavior does not eventuate in slavish obeisance to the environment. Furthermore, the patient must perceive that his suffering is self-induced.

Jacobson (1971) discusses the technical difficulties created by the special transference problems of severely depressed patients. How is one to permit the markedly ambivalent transference of these individuals to develop sufficiently for analysis to take place, and at the same time, deter them from terminating treatment in resistance. This may happen after the patient comes out of depression because of a spurious transference success or because of a negative therapeutic reaction, that is, with a severe depression resulting in withdrawal from the analyst. Jacobson asks: "Can we avoid or do we promote such results by gratifying the patients' need, first for stimulation of their vanishing libidinal resources then again for an either punitive or forgiving superego figure?"

With respect to frequency of sessions, though the prevailing attitude has been to offer severely depressed patients daily sessions, Jacobson believes the emotional quality of the analyst's responses are more important than the quantity of sessions. The possibility of creating some degree of distance between themselves and the analyst reduces ambivalance. Daily sessions are experienced as "seductive promises too great to be fulfilled" or as "intolerable obligations which promote the masochistic submission." When patients appear excessively retarded during a depressive period or are suicidal, Jacobson suggests increasing sessions but handling this with caution: As illustration she cites a retarded, paranoid-depressive requiring 10 minutes or so to leave, though "later on she blamed me resentfully for having stimulated her demands by the 60-minute sessions."

Jacobson feels there must be a "continuous, subtle, empathic tie" concerning analyst and depressive patient. She cautions against permitting empty silences to continue, suggests the analyst not talk too long, too rapidly, or too emphatically, "never to give too much or too little." Required by these patients is not so much longer or greater number of sessions but warmth, spontaneity, attunement to their mood, and, especially, respect. These are not to be confused with "over kindness, sympathy, reassurance." During times of imminent narcissistic withdrawal one must evidence active involvement in their everyday life and, particularly, in their sublimations. Occasionally, "supportive counterattitudes and interventions are indicated" but are employed as a "lesser evil." All this notwithstanding, depressive patients intermittently may feel the analyst's attitude as "severe rejection, lack of understanding, or sadistic punishment, all of which may increase the insatiable demands, the frustration, the ambivalence and ultimately the depression." The most precarious point is the patient's temporary need for the analyst's "show of power." That is, "at critical moments the analyst must be prepared to respond either with a spontaneous gesture of kindness or even with a brief expression of anger which may carry the patient over especially dangerous depressive phases."

In working with severely regressed patients committed therapists endure periods of masochistic submission to their patient's aggression, exaggerated doubts as to their capacity, and fear of criticism by others (Kernberg, 1965). The analyst may identify with the patient's aggression, paranoid projection, and guilt: "Narcissistic withdrawal from the patient in the form of passive indifference or inner abandonment by the therapist and narcissistic withdrawal from external reality" in a reciprocal relationship with that patient are possible dangers, especially regarding analysts whose narcissism has remained unresolved in their own analyses.

In a later paper Kernberg (1972) suggests that in borderline patients there is an excessive development of pregenital and especially oral aggression that creates premature emergence of oedipal strivings and, as a result, a distorted fusion of pregenital and genital processes under the overriding influence of aggressive needs. In particular, oral aggression is projected, resulting in the paranoid distortion of early parental figures, especially the mother; the acting out of the transference within the analytic relationship proves the principal resistance or obstacle to further change. Setting up "structuring parameters or modifications of technique" are crucial as a "protective, technical requirement." To illustrate, Kernberg refers to a hospitalized, borderline patient who "literally yelled" at her therapist during their sessions. On noting that his patient seemed completely relaxed talking to other patients and with hospital personnel, the therapist concluded her angry outbursts at him indicated a gratification of her aggressive needs beyond any

available to her before hospitalization and that this gratification comprised a major transference resistance. As this
was communicated to her, and the therapist limited the
barrage of shouting and insulting during the session, the
patient's anxiety increased visibly outside the hour; her
central problems were externalized within the hospital setting. Changing attitudes in the transference emerged, pointing to growth in the therapy.

Narcissistic personality disturbances (Kohut, 1971) that
encompass anxious grandiosity and excitement, on the one
hand, and mild embarrassment, self-consciousness, severe
shame, hypochondria, and depression, on the other, tend to
create two types of analytic situations. Patients may establish a specific relationship to the analyst, using him as a
mirror within which to discover themselves and be reflected
in his admiration of them (the grandiose self- or mirror
transference). Alternately they may admire and idealize the
analyst, experiencing themselves as part of him, feeling
competent and strong in the event this experience can be
maintained (overestimated parent-image or idealizing transference).

In reaction to the patient's transference mobilization
of the idealized parent-image, the analyst—motivated by a
defensive rejection of his own painful narcissistic tensions—
frequently wards off the patient's idealizing attitudes. These
narcissistic tensions emerge when the repressed fantasies of
the analyst's own grandiose self become stimulated by the
patient's idealization. Actually, there is only one correct
attitude: to accept the admiration. The slow, disappearance of the idealizing transference, which occurs in the
working-through period, brings with it a second emotional
test for the analyst. The patient may focus on the analyst's
limitations, manifest contempt, and engage in attacks on his
shortcomings. This display of contempt alternates with a

show of admiration for the analyst and may eventually lead to a strengthening of the patient's internalized narcissistic structures or ideals.

In the mirror transferences, especially the twinship or merger aspects, the analyst as an independent individual tends to be erased from the patient's associations. This occasionally interferes with the development and maintenance of the transference and working-through process. The analyst's narcissistic vulnerability makes it difficult for him to tolerate a situation in which he is reduced to the passive role of being the echo or mirror of the patient's infantile narcissism. Optimally he should interpret the patient's resistance to confronting his grandiosity or demonstrate to the patient that grandiosity and exhibitionism once played a phase-appropriate role and must now be allowed access to consciousness. It is desirable that he accept his position within the patient's therapeutically reactivated, narcissistic world-view as merely that of an "archaic pre-structural object," that is, a "function in the service of the maintenance of the patient's narcissistic equilibrium."

Of interest is Kohut's discussion of the "traumatic states" that occur in the middle or later stages of the analysis of narcissistic individuals, often in reaction to correct interpretations that would ordinarily encourage analytic growth. Though one might interpret these states as pointing to unconscious guilt or reflecting a negative therapeutic reaction, Kohut suggests that narcissistic individuals are not permeated with guilt or superego pressures. They tend, instead, to be beset by shame—a reaction to the breakthrough of archaic aspects of the grandiose self, especially to its unneutralized exhibitionism. The analyst can help resolve these traumatic states if he perceives that they have to do with a flooding of unneutralized, often oral–sadistic, narcissistic libido. If the analyst communicates his awareness in "appropriately presented interpretations, then the patient's excitement will usually subside."

Salzman (1959) believes Freud to be unduly pessimistic regarding the therapy of masochism and feels Freud did not fully comprehend the dynamics of what is termed "the tug-of-war" phase. The success or failure of therapy is attributable to the active intervention of the analyst in coping with this situation, which fulfills, as well as exposes, the masochistic trends in an atmosphere optimally suited to explore them. This is contrasted with so-called classical detachment, which merely stimulates dormant masochistic defenses unavailable to analysis. A sense of bondage to an authority one must not challenge but concerning whom there is hostility and contempt is thus created. This classical analytic setting is then but a prototype for the "typical relationship" set up by the masochist in relation to his environment.

Salzman describes at length his work with a 25-year-old woman who presented herself as a "lifelong" victim of humiliating and self-hurtful experiences. She depicted herself as unattractive and inadequate, though in fact she was the very opposite. She sought to have her analyst believe she was an intractible person who had prickly, abrasive relationships with everyone and did not really deserve to be his patient. Concerning her briefly depicted history, it appears that she was eldest of two children. Her father, a successful businessman, was shunted aside in his role as husband and father by his dominating, complaining wife. The patient concurred with her mother's derogation of her father, though she argued and was at sword's point with her mother over everything else.

This patient functioned in a state of heightened anxiety and tension that proved a way of life. If this tension were absent, it resulted in further masochistic behavior. Salzman feels her personality traits represented the acting-out of a child who, because of early deprivation, seeks an unending amount of emotional supplies. Her needs were never directly stated, but, rather, she seemed perpetually whining, demanding, and contentious. When this did not evoke the desired response, she heaped abuse on the therapist or demanded that her suffering yield her tender, loving care from others. Even when it was forthcoming, she scorned or belittled interest and concern. The patient pervasively projected a theme of rejection, resulting in feelings of worthlessness and unlovableness. The therapist was inevitably cast in the role of depriving parent, insufficiently giving or caring.

Salzman indicates that these problems came to the fore approximately six months after therapy began, at which point his patient questioned the efficacy of their work together, testing the analyst's interest in her, as follows:

Patient: Have you been able to change my hour yet?
Doctor: Not so far, but I haven't forgotten about it.
Patient: It's terribly inconvenient, and I wish you would hurry up.
Doctor: (firmly) I'm doing what I can.
Patient: Should I feel honored or guilty?
Doctor: Let's hear what you do feel.

In this exchange, Salzman feels his patient viewed a situation that could have led to mutual decision making as one replete with denial and threat. In a rather open and courageous fashion, Salzman plumbs the depths of his internal ruminations, states he feels angry and coerced: his patient seeks to "make [him] . . . feel like a pompous, condescending prig who is doing her a big favor," instead of transacting a simple request. Because he is irritated with her tone or manner, his patient ascribes feelings of impatience, intolerance, and lack of analytic detachment to him. Salzman feels put upon and asserts: "Nothing can satisfy her. How can I help her to see this?" Salzman points to the emergence of feelings of "guilt, pity and professional pride" in response to his patient's thrust about being thrown out of therapy. He admits in a very human passage an inclination on his part towards doing just this, which he feels is the core of the patient's difficulties: her intense dependency, along with the concomitant need to ward off or deprecate any proffered help. He hazards the notion that most analysts dealing with the "masochistic defense" would respond similarly.

I do not agree. I feel Salzman's countertransference attitudes regarding this patient, who is no doubt complicated and provocative, is an integral part of the emergent therapy. Though angry, oppositional patients are indeed difficult and harrowing to work with, it is my impression that Salzman proved overly challenged and irritated by her demanding, imperious, peremptory attitude. One need not necessarily view her question about feeling "honored or guilty" as "sharp and cutting" as Salzman did. According to Salzman, the question "dug deep into the heart of the analytic process and its pretensions of objectivity."

Why not acknowledge that in the analytic situation the therapist has the upper hand; is the authority; is in the powerful position; and, after a fashion, exhibits largesse, in that the arrangements, especially fees and time, must, for the most part be convenient for him. He may try to accommodate the patient's needs, but the final decision is his: He may simply be unable to be a master juggler and arrange the time so that it is mutually satisfactory.

Salzman states his patient is a "bitch . . . forcing me to admit I haven't made the switch yet and am therefore neglecting her. I've already taken steps to make the change. It doesn't depend only on me!"

Why not avoid a stance of lofty detachment and tell

156   THE JOY OF SUFFERING

the patient one has "taken steps." In asking "Why is she never satisfied," Salzman might be introducing a note of "prophetic fulfillment," instead of exploring other situations where she feels similarly dissatisfied or disgruntled, perhaps in her relationship with her parents or helping her become aware of her quite considerable identification with the mother's derogatory attitudes towards father and the male sex in general.

Salzman indicates that for the remainder of the session, his patient conveyed that she felt the analysis was not reaching her, was not, as formerly, the most significant focus in her life. The patient related that her first analysis concluded along similar lines, that she felt her former analyst was "fed up with her."

The last exchange during this session follows:

Patient: I seem to be testing again, seeing how nasty I can be before getting thrown out. I would like you to get angry enough to throw me out.

Doctor: If you try hard enough you could probably succeed, but what will you gain from it? It does not necessarily prove that you are worthless but only that some of your acting-out can become intolerable. I have a feeling that you are not only testing limits, but testing me—to see how angry, irritated or nasty I can become.

Patient: (in an irritated manner) What do you want me to do? Go to another therapist?

Doctor: (I said nothing but indicated with a gesture that the choice was up to her.)

It seems to me that at no point should one indicate this patient could succeed in being thrown out. It is imperative that her resistance and its unconscious concomitants be dealt with. In the last rejoinder, where it was suggested that the choice of going to another therapist was up to her, Salzman could be inadvertently communicating his lack of care. The choice was also his to determine, and it would be crucial, in my thinking, to tell her she was not at all ready to terminate therapy. Of course, ultimately, the choice or actual decision was up to her.

Salzman feels the therapist is entangled in a double bind with this kind of patient. If he is reassuring and active, he is ostensibly undermining the patient's capacities. If he is firm, he is considered cold and distant. If he does not respond or intervene, he is accused of being passive and weak. Presumably this patient felt she needed no one, her integrity inhering in her own strength. This notion was reinforced, according to Salzman, by the "enormous manipulatory power which resides in the masochistic defense." Apparently, "others were constantly being pushed, forced and tricked into fulfilling her neurotic needs." One questions the so-called enormous manipulatory power, however, inasmuch as the patient does not in actuality get what she needs or deeply longs for. Also, if one pays more attention to the underlying needs, one is not as dazzled by the defensive structure.

Salzman points out that the manipulation is almost always "indirect and subtle" and is conveyed in nonverbal fashion; for example, his patient's tone of voice was frequently whining, hopeless, or accusing. Her expression was hurt and defeated. Of interest is his finding that discussions of the significance of nonverbal patterns were less controversial and argumentative than those concerning verbal productions. If an insight or breakthrough occurred, this patient would counterpose with a complaint or criticism of the analyst. Her more authentic feelings could be observed, however, by tone of voice or softening of her gestures.

Success or failure in the therapy of the masochistic patient, states Salzman, has to do with the analyst's competence in coping with the dynamics of the "tug-of-war" situation. Salzman feels that the struggle where the patient deflects every interpersonal exchange into a humiliating experience is inherent in the masochistic process. The therapist should directly intervene and externalize such exchanges. This results in direct involvement in the battle, precludes the tendency to submerge emotionally charged attitudes, and to continue the battle at a level inaccessible to analysis. Nonintervention does not avoid the tug-of-war. Classical detachment engenders considerable anxiety and evokes still greater masochistic defensiveness, which may go underground and prove resistant to further analysis. Therapy can remain pleasant and serene, but nothing may be happening. The patient may be collecting grievances regarding the therapist that never emerge and feeling enslaved to an authoritarian parent she cannot confront— the typical relationship she harbors in her relationships to others. This, according to Salzman, leads to the interminable analyses so typical in working with the masochistic personality. The active approach also takes cognizance of the masochist's need for contact and interaction; in effect it makes it necessary for the patient to examine her neurotic patterns in a benevolent atmosphere.

Salzman thus plunges into the fray, though it would seem particularly crucial here to keep one's cool, avoid defensiveness, and judgment, and, simultaneously, remain aware of the multifaceted aspects of the masochistic syndrome.

Though Salzman feels it is hazardous work, one need not view masochistic transference reactions with pessimism, gloom, or with the notion that patients with such traits are unanalyzable. One approaches these reactions as one would any other transference resistance, interpreting the resistances repeatedly, suggesting the patient view these as analytic problems. As for oneself, one seeks to be as neutral and objective as possible, to keep in mind the multiple role of masochistic phenomena, and to explore historic and dynamic implications when appropriate.

Admitting that it is difficult to preserve an analytic attitude when the patient's communications are replete with feeling abused by the analyst, whose attempts to communicate with and help him may merely exacerbate his problems, Brenner (1959) indicates that it is as relevant to preserve an analytic stance in this context as it would be regarding any transference resistance. For him, the decisive ingredient in the working-through process regarding masochistic patients is the "steady day-to-day work," with a sharp focus on the totality of conflicting forces within the individual.

He adduces clinical data to demonstrate that the presence of masochistic traits does not obviate therapeutic success. Nor does the degree of progress depend solely upon the severity of masochism present, he feels. This is evident in his description of two symptomatically comparable male patients with the masochistic components in one of them, Y., exceeding the other, Z. Y. manifested more overtly masochistic sexual conflicts having to do with masturbatory fantasies regarding beating and rape. Y. tended to feel more victimized in his social relationships than did Z., which actually had near disastrous consequences insofar as Y.'s career was concerned. Furthermore, he was exaggeratedly dependent on his parents, permitting them to disparage and beat him, even as an adult, whereas Z. was physically separated from his parents at late adolescence.

Z. described a pervasive sense of unhappiness and inability to fall in love and marry. Z.'s analysis persisted for years, evidencing a tenacious, unyielding, masochistic transference that fully emerged when unconscious, homosexual attitudes were elicited and eventuated in his wish to flee treatment. Y. swiftly became aware of and resolved homosexual and sadomasochistic attitudes. Symptomatic improvement proceeded faster for Y. than for Z., including more harmonious social and heterosexual relationships, positive work orientation, and increased capacity for pleasurable experiences. Transference resistances were resolvable despite the sadomasochistic nature of the fantasies.

Brenner shares with us his method of working with a complicated masochistic transference reaction by exploring a particular phase in Z.'s therapy. Apparently Z. sought a change in fee. Though this request was communicated in objective terms, his dreams and associations suggested that his longing for such a concession embodied an early desire to be the favored child in his own family, since there had been considerable rivalry with a younger sister.

It seemed at this juncture that Z. was working productively in his analysis. In actuality, he was seeking to gain a material symbol of the analyst's affection by this "good" behavior. On finally perceiving that his hope for a gift from his analyst was to be denied, Z. experienced a sense of intense anger, frustration, and exploitation; he felt if anything he had become worse and indicated he was terminating analysis. Brenner interpreted his patient's rage, desolation, exacerbation of symptoms, and desire to flee therapy, as due to his having linked frustration of his patient's request to similar deprivations in childhood. Though Z. did not then terminate analysis, Brenner found the facilitation of his patient's masochistic transference resistances hard going.

In working with masochistic transference the following are salient principles, according to Brenner:

1. The analyst should avoid expressing anger, resignation, defeat, affection, or aversion, or he would be unconsciously participating in the patient's sadomasochistic behavior.
2. The analyst must be cognizant of the complicated motivations of the masochistic trends so that he is alerted to these in whatever structure they emerge, however concealed, whether defensive, expiatory, unconsciously gratifying, or a repetition of the patient's mode of reacting to the instinctual conflicts of early life.

A paradigm for the analyst is that of an

understanding adult who had the task of dealing reasonably with a sulky, stubborn provocative child. If the adult is wise and not unduly involved with the child he is not upset or disturbed by such a child's behavior but remains calmly observant and understanding whatever may be the child's attempts to seduce and provoke him into a sadomasochistic episode.

The analyst, in working with masochistic and other patients, should be optimally competent, accepting, respectful, exploratory, interested, and committed. I do not feel it is a matter of role playing that one offers friendly understanding to counter the punitiveness or criticalness of others. This attitude should be deeply felt. There is no doubt that many analysts are bored, resentful, or angered by stereotyped repetitions and complaints, have minimal tolerance for the martyr-like perpetuation of self-defeating mechanisms, and for the denied hostile provocativeness of the masochistic patient. It seems to me this is acceptable and human, as long as it is not acted out and the analyst perceives and resolves this as countertransferential involvement regarding some past reaction to a resembled figure. Salzman's (1959) notion that his patient feels trapped by the analyst as an authority she cannot overthrow but for whom she has utter "contempt" is highly questionable. It is doubtful his patient harbored contempt; rather her hostility toward her analyst and her self-depreciation might incorporate a child's plea to be loved even though "bad."

The analysis of a primary ego disturbance in a patient with pervasively masochistic, as well as depressive and projective, features may best illustrate the vicissitudes and complexities of working with patients who display a masochistic lifestyle. Obviously, there is no one or ideal approach within the analytic situation. My patient F., in her history and development, manifests a good many of the mechanisms that recur in persons with masochistic formations. A unique disturbance in the needed mutual regulation of the mother–child relationship, emerged in the oral phase, as well as in later psychosexual phases, resulting in deformation of the ego, a pervasive degree of self-devaluation, underestimation of capabilities, and inhibition of activities.

F. sought therapy because of suicidal thoughts, headaches, lethargy, and her ambivalent relationship with her mother. Mostly, however, her highly troublesome sadomasochistic fantasies propelled her. F., who has been in analysis with me for $7\frac{1}{2}$ years on a 3-session-per-week basis, is 37 years old, Jewish, and unmarried; she came to the United States with her parents from Austria at age 9.

She is a college graduate, has lived on her own for the past 10 years, and is currently employed in a fairly responsible, supervisory position. When initially seen, she appeared indeterminate in appearance and generally wore fairly matronly clothing. Her parents, in their late sixties, still speak mainly their original language, and though they have lived in the United States for several decades, function as though encapsulated in their former lives.

What emerged as central in the long list of F.'s multiple complaints was her unresolved, symbiotic relationship with the mother. Initially overidealized and placed on a pedestal, her mother was someone toward whom F. could never feel critical, rebellious, or consciously hostile, since she feared separation. The mother was rarely direct or open in her behavior towards the patient. She masked her disapproval and anger, presented herself as long-suffering and martyred, and was herself a mother-attached, masculine woman, who tended to parentify F. Generally, she formed an alliance with F. against her husband, facilitating F.'s rejection of her father and later of other men. F. felt her father was an ineffectual, narrow, distrustful, methodical man. She hated him because she felt he was ridiculing, uncaring, and did not protect her sufficiently. She blamed him for her parents' difficulties and felt bitterly the mother's pretence of deferring to him. Her father was essentially devalued by her mother on coming to this country; the maternal uncle was elevated to head of the family.

As mentioned, F. experienced suicidal thoughts at this time, facilitated by her mother's need to prove that F. could not succeed at anything and augmented by maternal pressure to get married. That is, her mother would intrusively call girlfriends to inquire about F.'s possible dates with men. F. experienced this as assaultive and humiliating, as well as rejecting, since her overwhelming need was to preserve the symbiotic tie with her mother. She was afraid to tell her mother to stop calling friends, as this would externalize the dissonance between them and might result in separation between herself and her mother. Because her mother's sneaky behavior had become more and more intolerable to the patient, my first therapeutic task was to help F. ventilate her anger toward her mother with me and to encourage her to tell her mother to cease being so invasive.

F. was born in a fairly small town in Austria and lived there until she was four with her parents and paternal uncle's family, which included a daughter several years older than the patient, with whom she was unfavorably compared.

In early infancy F. was hospitalized twice because of "feeding difficulties." According to the mother, her physician felt F. and mother were "not good for each other" and required separation for a short period. There is the suggestion that following this period of rejection the mother then sought to engulf or infantilize the patient and that this early oral syndrome, with its alternation of excessive frustration and excessive overconcern, proved the basis for F.'s later sense of traumatic deprivation. As noted, many patients experienced similar mother–child constellations in their early years.

During this period, the maternal grandfather died, and F.'s mother became quite depressed. F. indicated that her mother had hoped for a boy to name after the grandfather. Her maternal grandmother was warmly remembered as a jolly, old-fashioned, benign figure; her father was manager of a restaurant and recalled as kind, smiling, and affirming. F. felt her mother was threatened by the separation engendered by the advent of school and held onto her. There is an early memory, perhaps her earliest, of being alone with father in the bedroom; he related that she need not go to school that day because the synagogues in their town had burned down. Shortly after her father was placed in a concentration camp for six weeks. During this period, F. slept with mother, taking her father's place. She felt abandoned by her father, confusedly thinking he was a Nazi.

When the family left Austria, the maternal grandmother had to be left behind. The patient felt instrumental in her grandmother's later death in a concentration camp, as though the grandmother would have lived had she, F., not taken her place. The feeling grew that should mother and child be separated, one or the other would inexorably die. After talk of sending F. alone to France (this plan was dropped) and then almost being separated from her parents in England, where they first traveled, the family came to the United States. They were sponsored by the mother's older brother, a physician, who had found for the father the modest, low-salaried position he now holds as stock clerk. The mother worked as a governess, living with a family and taking care of two male children. Later on F. felt she and father were like children, competing with these boys for her mother.

F. lived with the uncle and his family, which she hated because of the stormy relationship between her uncle and aunt. Indeed, she often felt her aunt was like the proverbial witch in a fairy tale. Feeling utterly abandoned by her mother, whom she saw for a mere hour or two every other week, F. was convinced this had come about as some sort of punishment because she was "bad" or not a boy and that her mother favored the children in her care. She visited her father weekends, sleeping in the same bed with him in his rented room. Her father seemed distant and preoccupied; she remembered somehow feeling disappointed in him. This arrangement lasted for a year. F. felt estranged, homeless, and ridiculed by her peers since she couldn't speak the language very well. She had changed her name and felt she had changed her identity, that something had been decisively cut off in terms of the continuity of her life.

The family was reunited afterward, sharing an apartment with another relative. F.'s mother slept with the patient, now aged 10, and relegated her husband to the living room. This proved an enormously significant period for F. She and her mother had a hot-house relationship, from which everyone else seemed excluded. They were together constantly. Her father worked nights, and F. saw no friends, enjoying the physical, tactile closeness with mother. The patient recalled that her mother would undress in the corner of the room they shared, with her back turned toward F., as though hiding the front of her. F. vaguely felt her mother had a penis, and she too would have one.

There is no doubt that the early oral trauma was revived by mother's abandonment and that the patient desired this infantile, tactile relationship as much as mother did. One might conjecture that the disappointment described earlier in relation to sleeping with father referred to her regret in not having a baby with father. However, it is probable she also wished for a tactile closeness with him, from which he withdrew.

Because of the unresolved fixation on mother, it is doubtful that F. entered the pubertal phase of development at that time. Certainly she did not according to Freud's notion that one seeks to master the Oedipus complex at this phase or in terms of Helene Deutsch's (1944) concept that, optimally, the adolescent girl seeks to give adult form to the earlier, primitive tie with mother and thus end all bisexual wavering in favor of a definite heterosexual orientation.

F. recalled that at age 13, when her menses started, the sleeping arrangement with mother ceased, and mother and father were together once more. Here feelings of desertion regarding her mother and jealousy of her father were marked. Her bitterness and rage regarding the cessation of this relationship knew no bounds and had to be worked through again and again in analysis. My suggestion that mother's decision to return to father was a healthy one and that the previous pattern was guilt-ridden and abnormal was responded to with disbelief. F. felt she had been assuming the role of husband with her mother, and that her father was cast aside because he was inferior. Now her mother chose her rightful husband only when it became apparent F. would not acquire a penis, that is, when she started to menstruate. F. felt her mother "double-crossed" her; she felt humiliated in not having a penis. Her genitals, she thought, were "ugly, dirty, hideous, grotesque;" also repudiated were other delineations of her femininity.

An operation on an abscess in her throat, performed at home, led to a complex of feelings that she was in some way both raped and castrated, her body damaged or mutilated. Both F.'s mother and the doctor fooled her as to what was actually occurring.

Her mother had, incidentally, informed the uncle rather proudly of the onset of F.'s menses. F. felt that her mother "betrayed" her to the uncle who, after this announcement, proved sexually provocative when, on one occasion, she was alone at home. Ostensibly, he "soul-kissed" her, reinforcing her fears of oral penetration or rape, evidenced in repetitive dreams. One such dream follows:

Like a nightmare. I had to have an operation. There was a doctor and he said my appendix had to come out. I was terrified. Then I was sitting on a couch. In back was a man, a doctor, doing something in the girl's mouth as though extracting a tooth. . . .

Associations to the dream had to do with (1) fear of having been raped by uncle; "he had a penetrating stare . . . could tell I was menstruating. Being a woman is something to be ashamed of, to hide, be vulnerable to being attacked by men;" (2) an appendectomy or operation suggests something is removed; also, one is exposed or opened up; (3) sexual associations, i.e., "penis withdrawing, he wasn't extracting but hammering, suggesting movement of penis . . . or its force."

In relation to the analysis, the dream pointed to fear of losing the penis, that is, her masculinity; fear of being penetrated by the analysis; fear of her femininity, fear of losing her mother. The uncle attempted another overture when F. was older and, after his divorce, wished to date her. The parents never remonstrated with him, and F. felt they were his accomplices. The uncle was a promiscuous, hedonistic man who had been involved in a number of damaging situations with younger females, which were publicized in the newspapers during his divorce. Also, he tried to date her friends and examined one who had consulted him regarding an abortion. F. was hazy as to whether he had once asked her to undress during a physical examination. Paradoxically, despite her repugnance for her uncle, F. cared a good deal for him. He was cultured, lively, and interested in her as she felt her father was not. Actually, she was jealous of his numerous girl friends. She was frightened by her feelings of sexual arousal regarding her uncle and feared she could be a prostitute or was over-sexed. There is no doubt that later associations of suffering or pain with sex and pleasure had to do with the need to punish herself for the incestuous feelings regarding this father-image.

The patient's masturbatory fantasies started after an episode in school where the gym teacher asked the girls to show their underclothing. F.'s fantasies generally had to do with two females in a sadomasochistic interaction: the aggressor forces the passive partner to undress and then masturbates her. According to F., undressing before another is the height of humiliation. These fantasies continued throughout adulthood and are referred to as her chief source of humiliation. They ceased for the most part in the latter phase of therapy.

F.'s fantasies suggest an identification with both the aggressive and passive partner. In her associations, she fused aggression with masculinity, torture, subjugation, with her uncle, with rape, and with Nazi behavior. On coming to the United States, she saw innumerable World War II films concerning the German atrocities and felt sexually excited by them. Because she thought these fantasies and responses to be perverse, she felt as sexually deviant and pathological as she considered her uncle to be. When I sought to elicit heterosexual fantasies that were rarely offered, she usually described a sexual encounter where she felt humiliated or castrated; for example, her male partner would cut off the hair on her head, would shave her pubic hair, or would manage in some other form to abuse her.

F.'s adolescence was characterized by intense relationships with girlfriends who took her mother's place. She was thereby punishing mother for throwing her out. With these friends she occasionally felt sexual attraction. There was no interest in males except in an oblique way, that is, with the boyfriend of a close friend. The sadomasochistic ups and downs of a particularly destructive, triangular situation persisted for 3 years, when the patient was between 18 and 21. If she had a penis, F. thought, her girlfriends would not leave her for a male.

From 22 to 27 there was a bleak, empty, prolonged relationship with a young man, R., whom F. essentially felt contempt for; yet she claimed to "enjoy" his sadistic or forceful role with her in sex. F. felt R. used his penis as though it were a weapon. She felt highly vulnerable when he would touch her vagina, and she would achieve orgasm; she felt this as a loss of control, as being helpless or subject to his power. The concept that the masochistic patient in his imperative need for love, accepts abuse and ill treatment as though they were love, seems relevant to F., as does the notion that if one receives punishment in advance, then pleasure may ensue.

Were she to have a penis, F. felt, she could control her aggression as R. did, be "on top of the world." Women "must fight to get what they want."

An affair with a married friend, G., the husband of a close girlfriend, continued for several summers after the previous relationship ended. Though G. was a warm, giving man, F. felt not as much sexual pleasure, compared to the "excitement" experienced via the self-debasement with R. By "excitement," she meant a need for a high tension level, as well as a need for stimulation and sensation. She felt angry when G. broke off the relationship, despite the fact that she knew he was unavailable. F. also felt betrayed by me because I tried to point out her need to feel both victimized and revengeful toward men. According to F., I take the other's side or prefer others to her, as her mother did in unfavorably comparing her to her friends or in taking care of male children; I should unconditionally support her.

Insofar as the course of analysis was concerned, the second phase of our work together evidenced the following: (1) A deepening of her anger toward me for not taking her side; (2) an intensification of her fear of penetration, which could mean coming to grips with her feminine role, linking me (the therapist) with her uncle, who had a penetrating stare and could see through her or knew what was happening in terms of her body processes; (3) considerable fear of losing her mother and an emerging conflict between mother and analyst; (4) feelings of physical attraction, love, and dependency regarding me, as well as feelings of rejection, because growth could mean separation, and because I see other patients and have a family. This was not as exclusive a relationship as F. wished for. Her mythology indicated that so long as she did not have a boyfriend, she would magically have the analyst to herself. Overidealization alternated with a somewhat paranoid-like suspicion of me, that is, I might be perceived as dictatorial or could be spying on her.

The third phase of therapy had to do with the unfolding and attempted resolution of her identity struggle, something frequently noted in masochistic individuals where one's true self is submerged to accommodate another. On one level this problem is shown in F.'s inability to feel herself as a person separate from her mother. She envisaged her mother as "someone who envelops me, wants me to herself, wants me in her womb, to be attached to her in an almost physical manner so I can't get away. Our bodies seem fused into one. Feel I'm nothing . . . floating in space." Or, at times F. felt like an embryo, needed to feel she was in an enclosed room, and claimed to frequently experience this in my office. When she purchased clothing, F. used to have to remember she was a woman of 29, not an older woman and not an adolescent. She would choose clothes more appropriate to a girl of 15 or to a woman of 50. There were occasions when she heard her name and did not recognize it. Also, she likened herself to Oscar Wilde's fictional character, Dorian Gray, who feels superficial on the outside, diseased underneath. If she developed a self, she felt she'd have to give up the other person: "If I let go, I'll die."

At this time F.'s profound confusion concerning her sexual role was externalized in an intense relationship with a girlfriend, K. In exploring this relationship, the patient became more deeply aware of her need for total acceptance by K., her need to control K.'s life, and K.'s resentment over this. The patient decided against any sexual definition of this relationship, probably because of her fear of rejection. Again, F. felt that had she a penis, K. would not leave her. A penis would give her life aggression and identity. It would be the "miracle," she said, that would make her a person. F. subsequently yearned for more privacy and self-hood when K., in her turn, became too engulfing and demanding. For the first time F. became aware of her need for private areas of her own.

The two endlessly experimented with alternating male–female, husband–wife, mother–child, and dominant–subordinate roles. For the most part, this relationship proved constructive for F. compared to previous ones, since she could feel free to be more self-assertive. Despite her initial feeling of being unmoored when the relationship with K. was over, the analytic process was thereby catalyzed, resulting, at first, in her turning toward me with renewed demands and, then, in her turning toward men. Because of the patient's constant oscillations during this relationship, my task at first seemed to be one of helping her accept her homosexual attitudes, at least to achieve some temporary stasis. At times F. felt I was forcing her to choose between homosexuality and heterosexuality.

The identity struggle now devolved on becoming an individuated person and being identified with the feminine role. In the past, being responsible meant being a man, taking father's place. F. no longer wished to be a husband to her mother, or to be in a game where she and her mother were the parents and father the child. Currently she felt more and more that she was the parent and her parents were her children. There was a burgeoning sense of self, despite her back-and-forth desire to be the child again.

Concerning her womanhood, F., for a long period, felt quite mystified as to how to go about this, though she had begun for some time to dress more seductively and to look quite attractive. She could not identify with her mother, whom she envisaged as masculine, phallic, or maternal, but not as a female. She formerly identified with her uncle and had become head of the family when he died or had identified with father in feeling rigid and paranoid or in resembling him physically. In her fantasies, as well as in her relationships with others, F. had either been mother, child, or male. She felt herself to be a "neuter," a "monster," a "freak," a "cripple," a mixture of male and female. Since childhood, there was always the possibility of turning into a male, that is, a phallic female. "When I feel masculine, I feel it's wrong. When I feel female, I feel peculiar. I don't know what to feel." When she seemed in despair of changing or of being able to relinquish her fantasy of being the male aggressor—in context of her increasing desire to acquire female identification—I suggested she try to identify more with the female in her fantasy, who is in the passive role.

F. became somewhat less judgmental and critical of men. She had a brief, unsatisfactory relationship with a male co-worker, where she enjoyed the feminine role more than in previous heterosexual relationships. Feelings of retaliation raged after the relationship ended, though she herself precipitated this by her sense of urgency and desperateness.

I then became the patient's sole or primary love-object; she held on to the fantasy that her world revolved around me during the three hours weekly we saw one another and felt that I existed solely for her. According to her fantasy, I had no other significant relationships. Because I felt she could now accept reality confrontations to a greater extent, I communicated to her emphatically that I could not nurture her fantasy that only the two of us exist for each other. She must consider me and my needs. This implied that she too could become a separate, autonomous person and that separation could be considered positive and life giving. Naturally, this resulted in her feeling rejected by me. I was punishing her for her sexual interest in me, she claimed. I tried to have her experience me as the good mother who could bear separation, which her mother could not, and to reassure her I was not throwing her out. After all, I'd been there for seven-and-a-half years. I also imparted I was not frightened by her sexual interest and was glad her sexual feelings were coming through. We could compare them to sensual feelings she experienced towards her mother as a child; perhaps they were a bridge to later, sexual relationships with men.

We also worked through the anger and rage underlying her feelings of desertion; hitherto she'd felt that should she express her real anger, she'd be abandoned. She'd felt the need for years, she indicated, to scream out "don't leave me" to her mother. Also, she'd been frightened of her anger toward me because it was sometimes sexually stimulating, and this could mean she was a lesbian.

At this point, her father required hospitalization and was operated on for a prostate ailment. She perceived her father as more human, as having emotions, on seeing him cry. This, together with a greater receptivity to relationships with men and a generally more realistic, empathic view of them, resulted in a reconciliation with her father. She resurrected the kind, loving, oedipal father of her childhood and was now jealous of the closeness she realized her parents shared. What was distilled from the feeling of acceptance and love for her father was that now he could become a prototype for heterosexual love objects. She still found it was quite impossible to identify with her mother, the next step in resolving the oedipal phase.

F. became preoccupied with her parents' eventual death and realized there would be no one to take care of her if they died. At first, she wished to be their baby again. Being a woman was equated with being an adult, making decisions, entering a relationship with a man. There was a considerable degree of identification with a girlfriend who liked feeling feminine, which at first F. could barely comprehend. Finally, the patient indicated that she too wanted marriage, a husband, and children, and felt starved for male companionship and sex. Recently, she met and dated someone she feels she does not have to play games with; he is natural and giving. With him she has had orgasms in intercourse for the first time. He has asked her to marry him, and she has consented. She currently manifests considerable insight into her problems, has a greater sense of sexual definition, and, though there are neurotic interactions in the new relationship—namely, her difficulties in expressing assertive needs—they are benign, and she is relating to a man in a more meaningful, giving, and feminine manner.

Diagnostically, one might characterize F. as someone who, because of her mother's early depression and distance and then anxious overconcern, experienced emotional deprivation at the oral level, eventuating in a primary ego disturbance or deficit and setting up later distortions in object relationships that prevented her from developing an independent ego. Characterologically, the patient's masochistic, depressive, projective, and psychosomatic tendencies fit into this context. Despite the symbiotic tie of F. and her mother, a semblance of an early, oedipal relationship with her father seemed evidenced. The sequence of crises during pre- and early puberty seemed to fixate the patient in a complicated network of events where first a regression to an earlier, incomplete resolution of the phallic or castration configuration seemed apparent, along with the mentioned regression to an even earlier, oral phase. F. seemed suspended in her identifications, oscillating between a fantasized aggressive, masculine role and a feminine role equated with feeling victimized and humiliated by men. The role alternations in her family reinforced her sexual ambivalences, and, of course, underlying this was her profound struggle concerning personal identity, where she felt she was "nothing."

According to Deutsch (1944) the association with persons of the same sex in adolescence provides a protective shield against a regressive return to the mother. The homosexual component, too, is then better resolved than when repressed and absent. Perhaps the patient's close relationships with girlfriends after age 13, where she secured some degree of mothering, prevented more deep-seated pathology up until the time analysis began.

A summary of F.'s transference manifestations are of interest. She perceived me at first in a vein similar to her view of doctors generally or her uncle, who could penetrate or see through or rape her. She felt she could be hurt or castrated in treatment, or she alternated between over-aggrandizement of me and paranoid suspiciousness. For the most part, there was reluctance to get well because of the fear of losing me.

Insofar as countertransference attitudes are concerned, I liked this patient, found her history both tragic and fascinating, and felt she was quite bright, that her capacities were markedly submerged. Regarding negative countertransference, I on occasion felt bored, discouraged, helpless, or impotent because of F.'s relentless avoidance of any change. At one point, I recommended group therapy sessions, possibly with me, preferably with a male analyst, to supplement our sessions. This proved highly anxiety-provoking for the patient. She felt I was killing her off, getting rid of her, throwing her out. She did not care to share me with anyone. Also, in a group with me, she felt I could spy on her as her mother used to do in questioning her friends. My suggestion was therefore repudiated. Significant in her getting well was the sheer amount of time spent in feeling sheltered and befriended by the analyst, the respect extended concerning her wish to resolve the symbiosis at her own pace. The so-called negative therapeutic reaction has therefore to be viewed with a new look. Though a stalemate or plateau may appear to be occurring in terms of action-oriented change, subterranean growth or changes we may feel are too minuscule to take seriously are germinating in the context of an overall corrective emotional experience.

One further point: I learned that what might not seem to me to be tremendous gains, were however of enormous significance to her, for example, acquiring a dog, learning to play the guitar, going away alone on a vacation, or taking a course. In order to placate her mother and remain in the symbiotic bond with her—and perhaps to defy her as well—she deprived herself of gratifying, autonomous ego experiences and was, during analysis, experiencing them for the first time.

Brief vignettes concerning two patients, L. and M., seen individually, and one couple, N. and O., seen individually and conjointly, follow. All show the importance of undramatic, prolonged, analytic work in coping with complicated personality structures involving masochistic formations and masochistic transference reactions. In L.'s case analysis covered a period of 10 years, in M.'s case 3 years, for N. and O., approximately 4 years.

L. had been in therapy for a year and a half before working with me. His presenting symptoms were numerous: physical complaints, deep dissatisfaction with his work situation, insomnia, fear of insanity, fear of dying, overall sense of isolation from others, as well as intense, burning anger towards the world. He deplored his quite respectable job as editor and wished to be a playwright; yet he despaired of ever being recognized, since the manuscripts he submitted were repeatedly rejected. Though he experienced considerable difficulty in writing, he continued, painfully, to do so.

The patient behaved as though he were on trial and must prove himself by his writing: "to my mother, my agent, and to the world." After achieving anything of a positive sort, he relapsed into depression, claimed he has no friends, was an "isolate," did not "let anybody love me nor do I love anybody." He manifested a deep-seated sense of worthlessness, weakness, self-loathing, castration, and fear of homosexuality. He had dreams of drowning, of being disabled and scarred, and felt markedly inadequate as a male and as a person.

L. felt deeply ashamed of his father, whom he considered a failure. His earliest memory is of his father fainting when his business went bankrupt. After the economic upheavals of 1929, his father was only intermittently employed, and the family almost broke up. Aside from gastrointestinal distress, his father had numerous breakdowns and would on occasion threaten to kill himself; once in an argument he told the patient: "You're no good, you'll never be . . . you always were a failure and always will be!" L.'s father preferred a younger brother who is considered better-looking, physically superior, and an excellent athlete, whereas L. was merely the scholar of the family. L.'s attainments were resented by his father, who did not attend his son's college graduation exercises. The patient was extremely fearful he would "end up" like father. Of interest is a recurrent dream he recalled from age four of an ugly, crippled man, pulling a wagon down the street, chasing him down a cellar. The patient felt the man would kill him.

Mother had to work to help L. finish college, presumably scrubbing floors. His sense of guilt and need for atonement regarding his mother was marked. He felt his mother never had any life with father and remained in the marriage solely because of him. He feared he ruined her life by his very existence. There was tremendous overevaluation of his mother, who used him as a surrogate husband, discussing his father's sexual inadequacies with him. His mother linked the patient with a beloved father who died when she was a child and wished that her son go beyond his father.

Despite L.'s idealization of his mother, there was a pervasive fear of abandonment by her. He felt he was essentially unwanted, since his parents' marriage proved so destructive. The patient claimed there is a "telephone line" between his mother and himself, suggesting their symbiotic attachment. His wife was similarly placed on a pedestal. His in-laws were an adoptive family for him, probably because of their wealth and the prestige accorded his father-in-law. Yet he felt "kept" by them. For the most part L. dissociated his anger and ambivalence regarding his wife.

L. was able in treatment to resolve his dependency relationship regarding his mother, perceiving her more realistically as a guilt-provoking and dedicated martyr. Significant dreams in therapy have dealt with themes of breaking away from mother and metamorphosing from girl to man. L. no longer responds with such alacrity to the anxieties, disasters, and burdens, especially devolving on his father, that his mother seeks to thrust upon him. Nor does he go into the usual tailspin of despair in hearing about his father's latest self-destructive exploits.

Regarding his boss, in-laws, and other authority figures, L. manifests a more self-respecting attitude. He has also acquired a more commanding position with his wife, is less reverential, and, at the same time, increasingly aware of his unreal demands on her. A greater acceptance of his job and its potentialities is also present.

L. is able to enter relationships with others where the interpersonal level assumes more meaning and his inclination toward being self-debasing is lessened. He is closer with work colleagues. With one a good deal older than he, he is able to work out a surrogate-father relationship. His sense of masculine- and self-definition is altogether less precarious.

Verbal, sexual overtures he made toward me were used to show contempt for women and generally to put me in my place. Underlying these communications, once they were worked through, I detected feelings of warmth and a desire for closeness and friendliness. He was thus able to explore and resolve his masochistic, distance-provoking, alienating techniques in the transference relationship with me. Though he often proved abrasive, hostile, and provocative, I did not find myself bristling. At times I might indeed feel uneasy at his barbs or thrusts. Essentially I liked him, admired his sharpness, aliveness, complexity, analytic productivity, and his deep need to find and assert his identity. I hoped to help him close the chasm between his enormous self-disparagement and self-destructiveness, and his obvious capacity, however dissociated, for greater richness in life. Also, I am partial to literary folk and understand the background from which he emanates extremely well.

M. had seen a series of analysts prior to treatment and was on a heavy drug regimen. Her presenting symptoms were nightmares of an intensely terrifying nature, replete with "lights and noises," where she felt she could not manage to switch the light on. On awakening she felt "cursed" or "ugly" and called for her mother, yet could not make the sounds. M. is a beautiful and intellectually gifted young woman of 25 who has completely submerged her abilities in obeisance to the paralyzing barrage of almost psychotic anxiety she experiences in pursuing any semblance of work or study that could be productive. Each time she took a test or was expected to write a paper, she would break down.

She experienced a sense of degradation and hopelessness, practically apologized for living: "I feel lower than anybody." She was similarly beset in embarking on heterosexual relationships that could be meaningful, claiming she "blanks" with men as before a test: "With a man who is challenging, I become a dead head." She tended to choose men below her "caliber," who wanted her as their mother. Or she wanted them to be a father. She was overly preoccupied with her weight and had been on "diet" pills a good deal of her life.

M.'s core difficulties center on the symbiotic relationship with her mother: "I live only through her. I'm not totally living if she is not living. I have a great fear of her death. If mother dies part of me would die. There would be no life for me." Her earliest memories are of a blissful childhood, of sensuous qualities of "milk and honey," of "sunshine," and, then, of grayness and coldness when she was four, and the family moved from her birthplace. Though exceedingly bright and serious, M. could not read upon entering school, presumably because this would involve leaving mother. M. felt she was "everything" for mother, replacing what her mother needed in a parent.

Her father was "disgusted" and "repelled" by female children and would not have anything to do with her as she was growing up; he was irrational, authoritarian, and a severe disciplinarian. When her father slapped her, she linked this with being a "tramp," a "bum," or a worthless person. When she was 10 she recalled that her older brother was severely beaten by her father because he refused to go to school that day. Hiding in the closet, she was terrified by her father's murderous rage. Later, she recalled, her mother participated in this as well, though, for the most part, her mother stood up for her in relation to her father. In treatment, the patient linked her nightmares, described earlier, with her father's bad temper. M. never felt she could compete with her brother, who, according to her father, performed in a real and concrete manner, whereas anything she did was considered negligible. As a child she had fantasies of being in the woods with a group of boys who played with her sexually and tortured her.

The patient was fearful of working with me at first, because then her tie with mother would be severed. Also, her mother would not accept her illness: "If my mother didn't understand, I didn't want any other woman to understand. I'd be relinquishing her if I related to another woman. I would then become an adult." She claimed that when she is with her parents, she takes a "giant step backwards into the past."

The initial, as well as subsequent, working-through phases in treatment dealt with her conflicts regarding separation-individuation from her mother. The awareness that her mother was not an unalloyedly positive force became clear to her: "She often took the enthusiasm out of everything." She would tell M.: "Don't expect too much or you'll always be disappointed."

M. continuously perceived that her reluctance to grow or achieve—scholastically, professionally, or heterosexually—had to do with the inability to leave her mother emotionally. She sought to repeat the excessive attachment to her mother in her relationship with her roommate, though the latter was a more benign figure, proving quite willing to give her areas of privacy and independence.

With boyfriends she was overly clinging and encapsulating, so that she often succeeded in getting them to reject her. We constantly analyzed her role in these relationships, either in choosing unavailable men and then remaining in unrewarding situations or in so insisting on her worthlessness and inadequacy that she masochistically managed to get them to leave her. Though none of these relationships became permanent ones, she learned to communicate in a more equal and adult fashion and discovered an intense competitiveness with men, hitherto dissociated.

Another glimmering of change appeared in her longing for more meaningful achievement through work. M. had never been able to imagine embarking on such a course before, as it would interfere with her mother's conception of women as creatures who conventionally marry and raise families. Then, too, this would involve further, graduate studies, which terrified her. I encouraged her to explore her feelings about returning to school by taking one or two courses for purposes of cultural interest or enrichment in a subject she enjoyed, literature. Despite her enormous anxiety regarding reading, her gripes, and the readily produced impediments of writing papers, taking tests, and so on, she succeeded in getting through several of these classes over a period of two to three years. Then she finally took the plunge; after endless procrastinations she applied to graduate school and has been accepted. Concurrently, she is also in a more rewarding heterosexual relationship that, despite her inordinate distancing mechanisms, is apparently working.

How did this come about? Even though M. participated in one failure situation after another, both in the sphere of work and in her love life, subterranean growth occurred. Through analysis one simply perceives one's own and the other's behavior differently and each succeeding task is approached with less stereotypy and hopelessness. For example, a particular relationship might not work out, but one might learn and grow from it. One might react to rejection with more resiliency in the future. One need not simply view it as a failure.

In exploring my attitude toward this patient—though

184   THE JOY OF SUFFERING

it was often one of impatience because of her relentless sense of defeat—I found that I expected her potential eventually to come forth. I felt her verbal self-denunciations were not commensurate with what her capacities were. Though each step was, and is, fraught with considerable terror and anguish, M. is definitely oriented towards change.

N. and O., a married couple, were seen in individual, as well as joint sessions of psychoanalytically oriented psychotherapy. Ostensibly, they were engaged in "sadomasochistic" interactions. N. was often verbally assaultive and derogatory toward her husband. O. responded with passive withdrawal and paralysis. Underneath, both felt deprived, needful, ineffectual, functioned below their capacity, were enmeshed in conflicts regarding their respective families of origin, and were pervasively given to masochistic, failure-oriented patterns of self-devaluation.

N. likened herself to a "cripple" and felt the entire family was "fated to fail." Her presenting difficulties were headaches, diarrhea, minor accidents where she banged or hurt herself, inability to enjoy life, being out of touch with her feelings, feeling "unattached . . . floating without a frame of reference," the wish to reach her children, and be more loving towards her husband. This was difficult she claimed, since O. was weak, powerless, and without authority; he might ask their three-year-old son for permission to do something. N. indicated she did not wish to reenact the pattern of her family of origin, in which her mother would yell at and ridicule her father and he would "take" it.

N.'s mother is described as domineering, manipulative, powerful: "She can drive me to the point of hysteria . . . to a complete lack of control." Her mother visits once a week or so, and they are locked in a power struggle over the children, with mother bribing them and seeking to undermine N.'s authority. N.'s earliest memory has to do with being dragged to school crying hysterically, presumably over separation from her mother. She has a brother three years younger than she, and recalled her jealousy when he was born, especially in observing mother nursing him. This is exacerbated by the fact that N. was shunted onto a nursemaid. There was considerable rivalry, competitiveness, and beating up of her brother until adolescence. He was often the one punished for their quarrels. N. felt she was a "bad girl" as a child and embarrassed her mother a good deal: "She didn't like me at all. I did bad things. I didn't eat, was cranky, defiant, would nag, yell, have tantrums." Though N. frequently bullied her mother into acceding to her whims, she felt depressed when she won. Her mother criticized her friends, clothes, appearance and was forever comparing her with others. She felt her mother preferred her to be incompetent and dependent on her, and in a sense she accommodated her mother by not finishing college. She felt hopeless with regard to professional competence; she felt that she never finished anything. N. would like, however, eventually to pursue a career.

There was a semblance of relationship with her father until she was five or so. He helped with homework and took her brother and herself on pleasurable excursions. Then an abrupt change took place, and he became inaccessible and remote. N. felt responsible for this withdrawal; more likely the relationship with her father was considered an act of disloyalty to mother, who she then sought to appease by detaching herself from her father. During N.'s childhood her mother was perceived as rejecting and depriving, then engulfing and overconcerned, occasionally threatening or punishing her with a cat-o-nine tails or spanking her. Once she wiped N.'s face in her urine. Mother was also somewhat eroticizing, encouraging N. to enter the bathroom when she was bathing. She told her she used sex exploitatively to "get things" from her husband. This alternating punitiveness and eroticization seemed instrumental in N.'s later sado-masochistic fantasies. One of these takes place in a hospital where she is on an examining table, naked, tied down, forced to have intercourse with, or rather be raped by, a group of doctors. The experience is both brutal and pleasurable. She likens sex to "undergoing surgery," feels used and humiliated, finds the "whole thing such a job," resents male superiority, and feels O.'s love is conditional.

N. married O. because she believed in what he was doing and longed to be as free and creative as she felt he formerly was. She does not know what she wants to do outside of being a mother. At times she feels like a small child and reproaches O. because "he hasn't given me anything to live through."

O. derogated the quite acceptable job he has, indicating his problems have to do with feeling unrealized in his career and his inability to take steps to resolve this. He claimed N. frequently sabotaged opportunities that may arise for him. Once she lost an application he was working on, and he was too "ashamed" to request another. Or, she criticized his work or called when he was working at his studio because she was lonely. O.'s father was severely injured in an auto accident while attempting to rescue O., then 1½ years old. His father's face was smashed and his legs broken. He developed osteomyelitis and lost movement in both legs. Told he had 6 months to live, he survived for 18 years after the accident. O. felt entirely responsible for father's accident and lifelong illnesses.

O. felt "ganged-up" on and excluded by his parents. He was alone a good deal of the time and constantly felt the need to make reparations to mother for "killing off" his father. His mother was perceived as demanding, undermining, ungiving, cold, and castrating. She would occasionally erupt and beat him up and had mild epileptic seizures. He was not permitted to bring friends home to visit because of his father's illness. Also, due to his parents' fearfulness, he was not allowed any participation in sports. Perpetually exposed to parental criticism, O. felt he could not do anything right. There was little contact between O. and his father; O. often wished father would die. He remembered a series of dreams, after his father's death, having to do with his father's deteriorating cadaver. Another dream had to do with O.'s being crippled and disfigured: "Hole went through leg and bone exposed." Still another involves a sniper, the police, and himself; he is shot at over and over in the neck and head—"a moment of extreme black abyss." There were also repetitive dreams of finding himself in a social situation with a girl: He is somehow humiliated or abandoned, or his companion ridicules him or becomes completely cold.

O. was markedly isolated and depressed when he initially encountered N. He was attracted to her liveliness and to her circle of friends. In the current marriage situation, he feels N. is embedded in the pattern of strong authoritarian women in his life; matriarchal grandmother, punitive mother, castrating mother-in-law, and N. He sees N. as strong and powerful, despite her marked dependency needs. He prefers that she be in the masculine role. Occasionally, when he suffers a recurrence of his lower back ailment, O. feels like a cripple. He then gets N. to give him the emotional succor his mother provided for his father. O. feels unwanted at home and used only for his services. He is unable to ask for things or tell N. he needs her without whining or feeling martyred. Whenever she is on the phone at great length he feels overlooked and rejected. N.'s mother, who completely takes over and encapsulates N.

during her visits, is also considered a threat and rival. The struggle between N. and O. is rarely openly expressed or communicated. O. feels N. is bitchy, provocative, and sexually unavailable. She humiliates him by proclaiming her verbal and intellectual superiority, correcting his language, completing his sentences, and making fun of his voice or body.

As a couple these two feel within themselves a sense of emptiness and deadness. They live in a state of mutual symbiosis, expecting that one will give the other the parenting or aliveness or rescuing so sorely needed by each. Each wishes to live vicariously through the other. Each brings to the marriage unresolved problems stemming from his or her respective family of origin. Designating their interactions as sadomasochistic is misleading. Diagnostically they manifest character neuroses with depressive, psychosomatic, and masochistic traits, with N. evidencing hysterical trends as well. Underneath her prickly, "sadistic" surface towards O., N. feels "childish," as though she "hadn't been born yet." Her distorted, unrealistic view of O. has had to do with her identification with mother's devaluation and contempt for father and her mother's feelings of victimization in her sexual role. Furthermore, there is her experience of abandonment by her father and anger at her younger brother for usurping the exclusive position she held in her family of origin. In her current family, on the one hand, she assumes the castrating or powerful role, as her mother did; on the other, she wishes O. to be as powerful as her mother was, so she may merge with, or live through, him. O., in turn, identifies with his weak, sick, crippled father; he has submerged his anger at his distant father and ungiving mother, directing it at N. via passive forms of aggression or mastery. Since his mother was the active, dominant parent in his family, he feels it is expected N. will assume this role, too, and in so doing will also provide him with the ministrations his mother performed for his father. O.'s need for punishment is marked; he constantly seeks to make reparations to his mother because of his intense guilt over his mythical responsibility for his father's death.

Regarding treatment of this couple, at first there had been a considerable disparity in each partner's commitment to change. O. had been highly motivated in seeking to resolve his problems concerning masculinity and potency. N. had been more interested in a tug-of-war with O., as well as with her mother, who was ever hovering in the background. Though N. is fairly placating and ingratiating with me, the power struggle exists here, too, in her resistance to change and in her insistence that I prefer O. Initially the following goals were set up:

1. To get from them what they wanted out of therapy and to set up a situation in which they are active participants, since they require such marked degrees of symbiotic merging with others to feel alive.
2. To have them feel in closer touch with their respective feelings, to be conscious of their anger, so that they may confront each other, me, and their children, especially as they are beginning to transmit the family pathology to the latter.
3. To externalize the schisms in the relationship, cloaked by their initial preoccupation with moving to another state or purchasing a house.
4. To help N. resolve the ambivalent relationship with her mother, in addition to working through the transference relationship with me.
5. To help O. actualize himself in his work situation and to be more in touch with feelings of competency and assertiveness.

During the first phase of therapy, there was a more open discussion of mutual grievances, with O. countering N.'s thrusts which he felt were inordinately provocative and humiliating. N. felt, in turn, that O.'s sexual overtures were attempts to manipulate, control, or bargain with her.

O., though frequently discouraged, assumed a more assertive role, seemed less inclined to withdrawal or passivity, and claimed to be more outspoken at work and firmer with N. He frustrated N. in not acquiescing to her wish to purchase a house, unless she tried to work more constructively on what he delineated as her central problems: her sexual hang-ups, her dependent, demanding relationship with her mother, her reckless spending. Though there were relapses to his former recourse to passivity or psychosomatic illness, he returned to the new base line fairly quickly. N.'s resistances were evidenced in her preoccupation with her previous therapist, in headaches, lateness, and in her feeling that I favored O. or disapproved of her cutting him down. She acknowledged, however, that he is growing and changing and makes sacrifices.

I tried to convey that both are equally involved in their interpersonal difficulties, that O.'s withdrawal and N.'s verbal attacks are equally vindictive and retaliative. However, it was quite obvious that O. was highly motivated in seeking to change, whereas N. was sabotaging O. and maintaining the status quo.

In what I considered the middle or working-through phase of treatment, N. showed an increased resistance or flight into symptoms; she claimed she felt "indifferent" about coming or felt "formal" with me. It became clear she required an oppositional or antagonistic interaction with another to feel involved. Her previous therapist responded to her provocativeness, whereas I did not. As O. departed more and more from his pattern of submissiveness, N.

became ill, dizzy, or had anxiety episodes. However, there was a sustained attempt on my part to explore her relationship with her mother, especially her mother's excessive criticism, rejection, and punitiveness. We also examined her intense rivalry with her younger brother: "He was dumb. I often couldn't stand him. Then I wasn't a problem. He became the problem." I felt N. consolidated with her mother against her brother and father, though underneath the alliance with her mother, N. felt incompetent and unlovable. Later N. felt she could bully her mother into doing whatever she wanted, yet she felt depressed after winning an argument or contest with her. Perhaps N. felt I would follow her mother's pattern in helping to maintain her feelings of omnipotence by excluding O. as she and mother had excluded her brother and father.

O.'s guilt and anger about his father's illness; his feelings regarding his mother's need to implicate him by accusing him of aggravating father's illness, in "not doing the right thing;" his need to atone by himself becoming an emotional cripple; were worked through. His mother blamed his father's death on O.: "If I was better to her, she could have been better to father. I was cold to her, got a lot of negative things from her, very little understanding." O. has linked his mother and N.; he views both as competitive, undermining, and martyrish.

A decrease in the bickering and recriminations between this couple and a greater affectional rapport on N.'s part were merely pseudochanges. What proved a genuine crisis or critical turning point in therapy had to do with an intensification of the power struggle between N. and her young son S. over S.'s toilet-training problems, his intermittent soiling, and N.'s fear she might harm the child. It seemed to me N.'s tolerances were particularly minimal at this point, inasmuch as she felt abandoned by her own mother who had remarried and therefore was not as pre-occupied with N.

At this time I confronted this couple with the destructive effects on S. of their marital acrobatics indicating that his continuing toilet problems were very serious indeed, especially since he would be entering kindergarten. In their preoccupation with their individual and marital hang-ups they were not sufficiently cognizant of their parental roles and responsibilities. N.'s need to control S., her need to perceive him as "stupid" or not as bright or verbally advanced as his younger sister, which seems intertwined with unresolved problems over her younger brother and men in general, were explored. It was suggested N. allow S. to handle the entire toileting process himself to avoid interjecting her feelings of disgust and rage. The imperative need for O. to assume a more consistently dominant role as family leader was pointed out as well, especially at this point, in view of the boy's perception of his father as extruded, devalued, and castrated, and his focus on his mother and maternal grandmother as the authority or significant parental figures. Both parents subsequently became more relaxed over S.'s bowel training, and the tug-of-war has diminished. S. is becoming more independent, is now considered a "fighter," and is relating more freely to other children.

In the final phases of therapy numerous qualitative changes have occurred: The angry exchanges have practically diminished both inside and outside the therapy sessions. N. and O. are generally better able to discuss and reconcile their differences. They do not have to use one another as vehicles for their frustrations in regard to introjects. The focus of N.'s life now resides in her current family relationships, not in her family of origin. She has become more affectionate towards O. and is not as resistant over sex. She is in a work situation she finds rich and rewarding. O. no longer feels "anger, hatred and disgust" with himself, feels more confident, is no longer a "listener," and enjoys talking about his work to others. Of crucial interest has been O.'s application for a college teaching position, an old dream in regard to his professional aspirations. He felt this could never be actualized because of his inability to compile a resume of his life that would illuminate his precarious identity: "It's like being born or reborn. Coughing up your whole life."

It seems arbitrary to deflect responsibility for "negative therapeutic reaction," onto the patient alone. More objective would be an overview of analysis as a reciprocal, collaborative relationship with mutual responsibilities that are unique for each member of the analytic dyad. In a model situation, the patient[1] should feel optimally motivated and work oriented, be receptive to alternate modes of behavior, remain in touch with feelings, and freely associate. The analyst should listen, observe, learn, interact, feel rapport, empathy and intuitive understanding; be flexible and nonjudgmental; and offer interpretations. A blend of expertise, warmth, naturalness, respect, innovativeness (not gimmickyness), and attunement to one's own emotional

---

[1] In order to do the analytic work, Greenson (1967) suggests, the patient must communicate "in words, with feelings, and yet with restraint in regard to his actions. He must be able to express himself . . . intelligibly with order and logic, give information when indicated, and also be able to partially regress and do some amount of free association. He has to be able to listen to the analyst, comprehend, reflect, mull over and introspect. To some degree he must also be able to remember, to observe himself, to fantasy and to report this." The patient must simultaneously "maintain contact with the reality of the analytic situation" and be willing to "risk regressing into his fantasy world." The analyst must be depriving and gratifying, maintaining distance and closeness to the patient at the same time.

responses is crucial. An awareness that the analytic relationship is unequal in terms of arrangements such as fee, frequency of sessions, appointment time, and other appurtenances of the analytic format would also be realistic.

The analyst's global attitude—including the sum of his countertransferences regarding his patient—are as decisive in affecting the course of therapy as are the totality of the patient's productions. It seems pertinent to view each instance of stasis or negative transference with a new look, depending upon the level or strata of the motivational hierarchy of masochistic behavior that is elicited.

Aside from the explanation of clinging to illness, need for punishment, death instinct, or tug-of-war in the masochistic patient, one might, in addition, view the masochistic transference reaction, on occasion, as an avoidance of separation, a lack of readiness to fully resolve the separation–individuation dilemma. This is indicated in the analytic work with patients F., L., and, earlier, with C. Finally, it should be remembered that masochistic trends belong to a characterological context that determines the prognosis, as well as the elasticity, of resolution.

X. Cultural Implications of Masochistic Phenomena

In group behavior there are many permutations of dyadic interaction where one individual exerts power over another. These may be temporary, specific, or appropriate to the particular situation. Where the power or authority is irrational or calculated to humiliate, injure, or inflict pain, and where there is considerable duration of this exchange, sadomasochistic variables are being introduced.

The genesis of masochistic formations is to be found in the family unit. To the young child, the parent is everything. Survival literally depends on the sustained physical care and emotional nurturance by parents. The parents are perceived as physical giants.[1] Their pattern of interest, attention, and capacity for emotional succor regarding the child, as well as their respective sense of self and manner of marital relationship, all are crucial to the child's ultimate style of development and maturation.

Exaggerated emotional attitudes towards the parents are frequently continued into adulthood. That is, parents, parent-surrogates, or authority figures may be viewed as omniscient or God-like and are worshipfully overexalted. Or they may be depicted as monsters, ogres, oppressors, witches, devourers, and ensnarers. In our culture, the extended period of infantile dependency, followed by a prolonged childhood and adolescence, imprints and reinforces on the child patterns of parental authority considerably beyond the point where the child may be ready to individuate. Ferenczi (1909) refers to this early period as one of masochistic or "pleasurable obedience" derived from the passive–receptive or submissive position of the child insofar as his early relationship to the parents is concerned. The extended period of physical dependence of the child may set up such marked emotional reliance on parents that it proves difficult for the child to pursue a more independent stance. Residues of the early pleasures of passive surrender and of being taken care of, cuddled, protected, or instructed frequently lead to almost masochistic enjoyment of or submission to the demands of parents. In this context maso-

---

[1] Y. saw his father as punitive, wrathful, and unappeasable and transferred these attitudes onto other authority-images where they did not necessarily fit : for example, onto his brother or supervisor who were benevolent, rather than despotic, authorities. Thus, this dream fragment : "I entered a huge temple with a monumental arch. The person who approached me was a giant, seven feet tall, a wrestler. He threatened me. Then there appeared a really big giant threatening everybody including the first giant. One of the giants attacked me, threw me to the ground, sat on me. . . ."

chism might be said to be an inevitable and normal accompaniment of the socialization process. Masochistic dependence on parental figures need not necessarily eventuate, however, in a crippling of the autonomy of the ego. The latter occurs chiefly when the preoedipal relationship with mother has been an ambivalent one, alternately depriving and guiltily oversolicitous, unattenuated by a more rewarding surrogate-mother or actual father relationship. This frequently causes primary ego disturbances. The child then interiorizes the parents' ill treatment, illusorily equating it with love, protection, or nurturance and unconsciously seeking similarly negative emotional responses in later transferential interactions.

In contemporary society, where the family unit is the skeletal one of parents and child or children with its inevitable exclusion of any extended kinship group, the interplay of parent and child becomes central. Freud has definitively discussed the hothouse, oedipal patterns that occur in the unfolding of the psychosexual cycle of development. In regard to masochistic patterns concerning the oedipal phase in women, he felt that anal regression, that is, the wish to be beaten, may be a frequent resolution of the desire to possess father.

In addition to oedipal patterns in the triadic family, the child may also develop a sense of isolation or exclusion, particularly from the parental bed, as well as from pairings other than sexual. With the advent of siblings, differential treatment may perpetuate preexisting feelings of vulnerability.

Parental personality, as well as the nature of the marital relationship, also assume a crucial role in the child's adoption of masochistic patterns. The effect of the patriarchal father on a child's psyche is perhaps most familiar and predictable. In this context, the term patriarchal may refer to a continuum of marital, parental, and social roles ranging from positive attributes such as strength, constructive or rational aggression, assumption of responsibility, decision making and leadership to the opposite polarity, that is, to attitudes of dominance, authoritarianism, despotism, sadism, or to irrational authority. On the benevolent side, the child generally perceives every level and nuance of his life as structured and ordered. Issues are overt, direct, and unambiguous. Husband or father is fulfilling a culturally sanctioned role (Lidz, 1957):

> It is usually the father in middle or upper class families who represents the family to the extra-familial world, establishes the family position in society, and forms the major source of the family's prestige, pride and self-esteem. Perhaps more than the mother, his friendly or suspicious attitudes toward outsiders cultivate the group attitudes of the family to the environment. To the child he is the first intruder into the child's feelings of unity with the mother and optimally the child should develop a sense of identification with the father—one of mutuality as against the rest of the world.

Regarding the despotic[1] father, prohibitions and rules

---

[1] To my mind the despotic father figure in all its variations—individual and cultural, in parent or husband, tyrranical ruler and fascistic dictator—is pathological, an aberration of leadership. Studies on the "authoritarian personality" (Adorno, 1950) suggest that a "basically hierarchical, authoritarian, exploitive parent–child relationship is apt to carry over into a power-oriented . . . attitude toward one's sex partner and one's God, and may well culminate in a political philosophy and social outlook which has no room for anything but a desperate clinging to what appears to be strong, and a disdainful rejection of whatever is relegated to the bottom." The authoritarian personality is completely out of touch with his inner feelings and must at all costs deny subjective weakness.

may be severely and shatteringly restrictive, decisions meted out in an arbitrary manner, brutally overlooking individual needs, creating infantilization, masochistic acquiescence, or catalyzing eruptions of violent rebellion. As husband, the despotic father may relate to the mother as though she, too, were a child, a possession, or his property. Thus, he deflates her value as a person, diminishing her in the eyes of their children, and reinforcing a strong sense of identification with the oppressed on her part.

Since the child's masochistic predilections may already have been embedded in the preoedipal phase of development, the patriarchal father must thus be viewed in interplay with the other member of the parental pair, the mother. Generally joined to the patriarchal husband is the self-obliterating, submissive wife. She is, however, far more differentiated in her role taking in a mobile country[1] such as ours than the cultural stereotype would indicate. This is, of course, contingent on such varied factors as class, education, and so on. She may wear a placating and self-effacing mask and use this subtlely to undermine her mate. This pretense of mildness may be used to avoid a confrontation of mutual problems.

She may enjoy her "passive" role, encountering richness and fulfillment in home, family, and friendships, serving as emotional core of the home for her children and as an indispensable support and helpmeet to her husband. Alternately, she may feel resentful and crushed, convinced that life is harder for women than for men. She may possibly feel that motherhood destroys her attractiveness to her hus-

---

[1] In American history in the periods before and during the Revolution, the role of women was similar to that prevailing in the mother country. However, the frontier period catalyzed what was eventually to become a more matriarchal conception of women.

band. Perhaps children were not what she initially desired: Childbirth was quite lethal in former times.

In relating to her children, the mother may assume manifest attitudes of warmth, strength, joy, competency, and responsibility. Or she may be neglectful and overtly or covertly hostile. Her children may be used for surrogate satisfactions, displacing preexisting personality conflicts or marital frustrations onto her parental role. She may seek to deny the demands of the maternal role because of excessive dependence on her own mother: that is, she might have experienced an insufficient degree of mothering and was herself exploited in having to assume a parental role in her family of origin. There might well have been enormous resentment of younger siblings. Therefore, she could be displacing ancient, unresolved rivalries onto her child or children. The role of females in patriarchal societies, the gamut of frustrations experienced in being a nonperson, have set up strongly ambivalent attitudes regarding the role of both wife and mother.

The heroine of Tolstoy's *Anna Karenina* personifies the modern woman in an embryonic state of social development. Anna goes through a complex metamorphosis that encapsulates the development of modern woman. She begins as an anonymous appendage to an authoritarian husband and moves to the point where she can herself choose whom to love and live with. Her choice, because of her historical epoch, is replete with suffering and tragedy. The society of her time could not permit her revolutionary behavior or her feminine independence.

Within the family constellation of a strong, dominant male figure and subordinate female, there are infinite permutations of marital and parental interactions affecting the child. One might say that where there is subjective acceptance and enjoyment of the strong male/passive female roles, there is a good fit, with positive effects on children. Where there is "pseudo mutuality" (Wynne, 1965), a preoccupation of family members with a fitting together into formal roles at the expense of individual identity, there is a fertile base for later pathology in the child. For example, in B.'s family the stress was on form and outer conformity. However, B.'s father undercut his spouse as both wife and mother, depreciating her worth as a person. He sought to be both maternal and eroticizing toward his daughter, which created profound disturbances of personal identification on her part. Following his early maternal indulgence—which served only to cut off the mother—he became, at the developmental phase in which B. began to express a sense of autonomy, sadistic and punitive. Later, she identified in part with her martyr-like mother, deeply distrusted men, and sought out or helped to set up repetitive, sadomasochistic relationships with them. She introjected the patterns of ambivalence provided by both parents, their criticalness and negation of her, as well as the depreciated images for identification presented by the devaluation of one parent by another. This launched her upon a masochistic lifestyle.

Contemporarily, the strong, matriarchal mother and passive–aggressive father dyad seems to permeate the American family. In psychiatry, this is fashionably considered the basis for a good many clinical entities, namely homosexuality, schizophrenia, the addictions, and so on. When we describe the female as strong and dominating, we conjure up a masculine, phallic woman, critical, contemptuous, and ridiculing of the father, possibly symbiotic concerning her children, who may be used manipulatively as substitutive libidinal figures. She creates havoc concerning the sexual role of both male and female children. Her devaluation of the father renders the identification process with him highly conflictual for her son. He may feel similarly castrated or overwhelmed by women. Alternately, he may be overly involved in rescuing or placating mother, as is the hero of D. H. Lawrence's novel *Sons and Lovers*. The daughter might remain fixated in an unresolved mother relationship inasmuch as the shift to father might not be permitted to take place. She may be forever plagued by underlying dependency needs. Identifying ambivalently with this victimized and phallic parent, she may, herself, choose a role as wife with implications for martyrdom, chronic dissatisfaction, role disharmony, and suffering. Positive components of the matriarchal mother are that the child needs at least one strong, authority figure who cares.

A weak father may engage in detached, passive–aggressive behavior and relinquish power as well as leadership to his wife, whom he may view as a mother figure. He may act brutally toward his children, seeing in them siblings he can bully, especially in their early years. Or, he may assume the role of a warm, maternal figure, when mother does not fulfill her obligations in this sphere. Though in the young female child, who is competing with mother, there may initially be rescue fantasies toward such a father, the child has eventually to cope with her contemptuous, angry, disappointed feelings. For the son, such a model is devastating not only in terms of distorted identity, but also in terms of the complexity of oedipal problems, especially the damaging overinvolvement with the mother, its configuration of infantilization, feelings of inner weakness, sexual ambivalence, and exaggerated fear of the father's retaliativeness and rage.

We may conceivably encounter two strong or two weak parents. Of course, as with all typologies, these dyads are merely convenient constructs interwoven with degrees of ambiguity and complexity. One must begin with the assumption, particularly in regard to women, of a unique role regarding the marital, and quite another regarding the parental, relationship. Also parents may alter their relationship with each other and with their children in different evolutionary phases of the family cycle. For example, a father who may initially exult in the exploratory activity of the infant may feel threatened as the child becomes older, whenever new financial and emotional demands are required of him, for nursery school, private school, camp, and so on—all the middle-class trappings of child and adolescent culture. He may feel displaced and competitive regarding his growing male child, especially if he had insufficient parenting himself, and expect his wife to make up for it. Or, erotic feelings concerning a pubescent daughter may threaten him and result in his withdrawal from this relationship. The mother too may have diversified expectations and predispositions regarding her child in the unfolding developmental phases.

Feelings of cultural alienation, together with social impotence, may bring out masochistic patterns in the male child and later the adolescent. The being who is not consulted in decisions vitally affecting him, who feels he is a tool manipulated by the powers that be—as in warfare or in certain occupations—may interiorize the inexorable helplessness of man to forge his own destiny and thus possibly reinforce a preexisting masochistic orientation.

It would seem from the exploration of the patriarchal family that women and children have been, each in their own way, "oppressed" members of familial and other cultural constellations. The occurrence in the past or in primitive cultures of matriarchal families, more and more pervasive in contemporary society, adds complexity to the patriarchal image of women. This patriarchal image refers to a cultural condition of oppression, that may be accompanied, however, by countless subjective elaborations of role. Matriarchal women may feel victimized by "weak" husbands. Within the patriarchal totality, there may be varying instances of woman's individual power. These complexities are crystallized in the original Garden of Eden scene. Woman was made from Adam's rib, a subsidiary being. But with the willful and fatal eating of the apple, Eve, in effect, began the process of civilization—and its discontents.

It is of interest that the term family is derived from the Latin *famulus*, designating servant or slave, perhaps referring to the role of child in the family in patriarchal times. This is also relevant to the topic of masochism. There is in the Freudian interpretation of the Oedipus legend a clouding of Laius' attempt to kill[1] his infant son. This deed acts as the prologue to Oedipus' act of unconscious revenge. Mitchell (1968) makes beautifully clear Jocasta's collusion in banishing the infant child, in that she embodies "sexual woman," passively acquiescing to her husband and lacking in maternal proclivities. Also delineated are the inter- and transgenerational patterns in the inexorable unfolding of the ultimate tragedy. Generally, and perhaps too narrowly, all responsibility regarding the vicissitudes of the Oedipus complex is ascribed to the child.

In ancient times it was commonplace, furthermore, to kill unwanted children. The theme of the unwanted or feared child exposed to die occurs in numerous sagas of various peoples. Parental cruelty is also a frequent theme in fairy tales, myths, and literature. In *David Copperfield*, a fictionalized autobiography, Dickens describes the afflictions of working-class children following the Industrial

---

[1] Bloch (1965) notes in her observations of a group of patients dominated by oedipal feelings that the parents are perceived as predominantly hating and destructive.

Revolution in England. Exploited by both parents and society, these children toiled in the factories for long hours and low wages. In our own era, we face the predicament of the "battered child." History repeatedly reveals instances of subtle psychological and material defeats of child by parent. Ariès (1960) indicates that the discovery of childhood as a distinct phase of life is a recent event in Western man's development. Until the end of the Middle Ages the child, as soon as he was weaned, was regarded as a miniature adult who competed, worked, and played with mature adults. Only the insistence on education and the emergence of a new attitude toward the family consolidated the child in his separate and now prolonged, childhood.

The implications of *famulus* as synonymous with servant or slave may also be applicable to the role of women, especially in patriarchal times and during the Middle Ages. Until recently, female births and deaths were often not recorded. Infanticide was a common practice in antiquity and was especially widespread for female infants. The "defilement" of childbirth is also considerably worse for the mother when the infant is a girl Among the Hebrews, Leviticus requires that postchildbirth purification continue two months longer for a female than a male child.

In most cultures and epochs, the father has decisive power over his female children. This is transferred to his daughter's husband when she marries. She then becomes, in a sense, the property of her husband, who, in some societies, had the legal right to kill her in the event of her infidelity, though he could have many wives if he so chose. The ancient Greeks reveal a profound misogyny: "There is a good principle which has created order, light and man, and a bad principle which has created chaos, darkness and woman . . . ," states Pythagoras (de Beauvoir, 1953a). The laws of Solon gave women few rights. The Roman code placed women under guardianship and asserted their "imbecility."

Christian ideology in the Middle Ages has also contributed much to the theme of the oppression of women. When Canon Law was set up, marriage was viewed as a concession to human frailty, incompatible with Christian perfection. Celibacy was enjoined on the priesthood, and the dangerous character of women more markedly emphasized. The fathers of the church proclaimed their abjectly evil nature. Woman was only an "occasional" and incomplete being, a kind of imperfect man.

The feudal husband was both guardian and tyrant. As a rule, girls were brought up rudely. Women had little education and were under guardianship of the father, who sent those who did not marry to a convent. The knightly love of the twelfth century and the exaltation by the Church of the cult of the "mother of the redeemer" may have softened women's lot, though on the whole, men in the Middle Ages held an unfavorable opinion of women. In the literature of the time women were accused of laziness, coquetry, and lewdness. Apart from queens, saints, courtesans, or special instances in court or in the arts—which indicated how much women could achieve under more favorable conditions—the positive accomplishments of women in worldly terms were few.

Since the Renaissance, the sequence of political, industrial, and economic revolution has resulted in a considerable degree of emancipation and equality for women, though throughout the long period of the Industrial Revolution women were severely exploited in the factories; more subtle instances of oppression are still with us.

Myths, literature, rites, religions, legends, and artistic expressions of all ages reflect, as do dreams, fantasies, free associations, and symptoms, unconscious projections of the multiple roles or guises of women. These will be briefly discussed here as far as their relevance to masochistic formations is concerned. Central themes that emerge emphasize the exaltation or celebration of woman as mother or instrument of redemption. Yet the "good" mother appears in contrapuntal relationship with the notion of the "bad," "evil," and "destructive" mother or the "fatal woman." Omnipresent are themes involving retaliation and revengefulness toward women, and these are often of a violent and degrading sort.

Illustrating the "good" mother or "Great Mother" theme, we have the myth of Demeter, who represents the source of life and nature, and is associated with nourishment and growth. She is the earth, manifest in mountains, woods, and sea. She can be queen of heaven, sky, and moon. Love is her symbol. Or woman can be a healing presence, embodying maturity and wisdom, as does the "Great Goddess" or "Great Mother" Sophia (Neumann, 1963):

> Vessel of transformation, blossom, the unity of Demeter reunited with Kore, Isis, Ceres, the moon goddesses, whose luminous aspect overcomes their own nocturnal darkness, are all expressions of this Sophia, the highest feminine wisdom.

The basis for such idealization or celebration of the mother lies in her fertility and creativity, as well as in the aura of bliss present in the oral-receptive or sucking period, when there is synchronization or mutual regulation between mother and child.[1]

---

[1] The celebration of mother may also have to do with the supremacy of women in the sphere of social and family organization, as well as in religion, in a hypothetical, matriarchal period preceding Greek and Roman antiquity. It is suggested that at this time goddesses or mother figures were the supreme deities and were defeated later by the

In Neumann (1963) there is a poetic discussion of the symbol of the "rounded vessel," in which "the woman contains and protects, nourishes and gives birth," as well as an emphasis on the unifying visual theme in primitive sculpture of breasts, belly, and genital triangle. Exaggerated buttocks or steatopygia represent a close bond with the earth. Woman's unwieldiness and bulk compel her to take a sedentary attitude in which she belongs like a hill or mountain to the earth, of which she is a part. The greatest mother goddess of the early cults was Isis, whose name means "the seat" or "the throne," implying the expanse of the seated woman's thighs and lap, on which the newborn sits enthroned.

In the Middle Ages, the image of the mother of Christ, the Virgin Mary, contains the most sacred and highly perfected image of woman, although a woman without husband or sexuality. The respect that haloes this undefiled mother and the prohibitions surrounding her suppress that hostile disgust that is mingled with the tenderness she inspires. As a receptacle for this hidden repugnance we find since the Middle Ages the figure of the hated mother-in-law, who embodies all the latent hostility for the mother proper. In many cultures, also, legends concerning the cruel aspects of maternity are conveyed onto the figure of the step-mother, who would, for example, have Snow White perish, threatened as she was by her step-daughter's blossoming sexuality.

There is practically no figurative image of woman that does not carry with it its polar opposite: Delilah, castrator

---

Olympian gods of the Greco–Roman patriarchal system. Matriarchal culture is characterized by ties of blood, ties to the soil, and a passive acceptance of all natural phenomena. Patriarchal society is defined by respect for man-made law, predominance of rational thought, and man's desire to alter natural phenomena, which constitutes progress over the matriarchal world.

and destroyer, and Judith, redeemer; Pandora with her casket of evil knowledge and Athena with her godly wisdom; Eve and the Virgin Mary, dark and light, exist side by side. Permutations of the feminine character are thus various and contradictory, replete with ambivalence and duality. Woman is depicted as both idol or servant, source of life or power of darkness, truth and wisdom or artifice, gossip, and falsehood, healing presence or sorceress.

Her fertility and abundance are counterposed to her role as ruler over night, cave, abyss, hell, disease, death, and the grave. She is goddess of war and the hunt. The earthmother engulfs the bones of her children. Death is depicted as a woman, and women bewail the dead because death is their work. The ancient fear that women generate life only to take it back again is crystallized in the image of the female exacting blood: The Hindu Goddess Kali, preserver and destroyer of life, holds in her hand a cranium filled with blood. Medea engages in the inhuman butchery of brother, children, and king.

Early phases of matriarchal cultures are, we are told by Graves (1959) and others, characterized by the custom of human sacrifice, which is related to fertility rites—another feminine domain.

Death-dealing aspects of the feminine are further associated with harpies, or sirens with wings and birds' claws. Ishtar, Astarte, and Cybele appear as cruel, capricious, lustful, powerful sources of life and death, capable of enslaving men. Others, such as Aphrodite and Artemis and specters like Lilith, the Lorelei, and Circe, reflect personalized forms of the primordial goddesses, suggesting that enchantment inevitably leads to doom. In the petrifying gaze of Medusa who can turn men into stone, the pre-Hellenic world projected its symbol of a "terrible" or castrating mother.

Another aspect of the "evil" woman emerges under the general category of *"la femme fatale"* or Keats' "La Belle Dame Sans Merci," the unattainable woman who is dangerously alluring and clearly a sexual challenge. Writers associated with the Romantic movement in literature—Byron, Baudelaire, Poe, Swinburne and others—find the epitome of what is beautiful in a linking of the female and the horrors of the charnel house. There is an exaltation here of the grotesque and deformed, beauty heightened by the perils of contamination, beauty enhanced by horror. The syphilitic prostitute or the lady caught in death pangs appear as key figures.

This Romantic tradition merges at its extreme point with a "sensationalist" tradition most evident in the works of the Marquis de Sade. Here, erotic cruelty, hysterical enjoyment of horror and the perverse, and admiration of crime are rampant. The degradation of woman reaches its culmination in passages of sadistic frenzy.

What impact do these shifting, ambivalent, prismatic, images[1] of women, briefly described here, have upon maso-

---

[1] Flugel's (1961) interpretation of the symbolism of mythological characters is of interest : The child projects "his own painful feelings and the accompanying aggressive drives" upon the environment, especially parents, who are by "virtue of temporal and spatial contiguity" recipient of these feelings. "The qualities projected onto the outer (bogies) depend upon the stage of development at which projection occurs, in much the same way as the manifestations of sado-masochism depend upon the level concerned. Thus at the earliest or oral stage the projected figures suck, bite, tear or rend; at the anal or urethral levels they are liable to flood the world with filth or water, or indulge in other forms of widespread and fierce destructiveness; while at the phallic level they castrate, mutilate and maim—all of these stages finding expression not only in individual childish fantasy but in frequently recurring themes of fairy tales and myth. Projections of this type are responsible for the weirder forms of childish phobias, which people the world with strange and sinister figures liable, as it seems to the child, to attack him in queer, malignant and terrifying ways."

chistic formations?

First of all, there is a considerable degree of superstition and fear concerning women, harking back to prehistory or antiquity, when little was known concerning the physiological processes unique to women. Even today many of our patients have an amazing scotoma regarding sexual anatomy. The transformation from girl to woman is far more accentuated than the corresponding development of boy into man, and the entire reproductive cycle—menstruation, ovulation, fertilization, childbearing, birth, lactation—has generally been shrouded in mystery.

Is woman then sorceress or magician? The myth[1] of the Medusa might even suggest, among other possibilities and interpretations, woman's hermaphroditic proclivities.

Women's closeness to pain (defloration, childbirth), the connection of menstruation in the child's mind with sado-masochistic fantasies concerning male violence or rape, the fact that we are born between feces and urine (de Beauvoir, 1953a), might create an ambience of both fear and repulsion regarding female physiological functions. In particular, there are numerous taboos surrounding menstruation. Thus, the day woman can reproduce, she becomes impure. Since patriarchal times, evil powers have been attributed to the female flow. One of the most extreme taboos forbids sex with the menstruating woman, or masculine energy would presumably be destroyed.

Does man find it repugnant to perceive the "dreaded"

---

[1] Arlow (1961) perceives the myth as a unique variety of "communal experience" and "shared fantasy." He suggests that comparative mythology deals with the "dynamic forces of the instinctual wish" as modified by the "operations of the ego." That is, analysis of myths and artistic expressions follow the same principles used in analysis of symptoms, dreams, and free associations, all reflecting attempts to resolve conflicts via the mechanisms available to the ego.

aspect of the mother in the woman he possesses? Often he feels compelled to counterpose the sacred and the profane, the maternal and the sexual woman. There is overevaluation of the mother as sacred figure with an ensuing need to degrade the sexual object. That is, where tender feelings prevail, there may be no desire; where there is desire, one may not be able to love (Freud, 1910; 1912).

Second, the mother may be viewed as the donor of bad or poisonous or insufficient milk. This is perhaps the outcome of early oral deprivation and disappointments. It can also represent any one of a great number of clusters involving oral trauma, with its sources in the rages of teething in the oral biting stage, the frustrations of weaning, or in an overall lack of reciprocity between mother and infant in the oral phase. Should mother simply delay with breast or bottle, a collapse of childhood narcissism might occur in infants constitutionally prone to a low tolerance for frustration or heightened stimulation. Or, the "bad" or "evil" mother-image may have to do with mother's actual inconsistency, perhaps of a sharply oscillating sort, as noted in the patients discussed in Chapters IV and IX. Here, the mother seemed, on the one hand, abandoning, guilt provoking, detached, depressed, and lacking in inclination for the maternal role; and, on the other, resorted to an overengulfing, exaggeratedly infantilizing or oversolicitous role.

F. was hospitalized twice as an infant because she received insufficient[1] or improper nourishment from her mother. After they were reunited, mother became excessively concerned about F. Later, the earlier abandonment

---

[1] According to the mother, her physician felt F. and mother were "not good for each other" and required separation. Of interest is the phase "good enough mother" coined by Winnicott (1958) describing the adequate, but not perfect, mother, flexible and responsive to the needs of her child.

reoccurred via a prolonged physical separation. Subsequently mother had the patient sleep with her. This hothouse situation lasted for a year, catalyzing or fixating insuperable problems concerning the separation–individuation phase, as well as every other phase. It was replete with pathology for this patient.

As mentioned, the theme of an ambivalent, essentially depriving, mother, repeatedly occurs in fairy tales: for example, the witch in Hansel and Gretel, whose house, i.e., exterior, is made of gingerbread and candy, but who, in reality, eats little children.

In the Oedipus myth, the sphinx is depicted as a female monster with woman's head and bosom, lion's body, serpent's tail, and eagle's wings. She throttles anyone who cannot answer her famous riddle and is a destroyer of men and eater of raw flesh. Balter (1969) has demonstrated that the symbolic meaning of the Sphinx in the Oedipus myth has to do with her representation as the maternal image of the oral–sadistic stage, that is, the cannibalistic mother. In Greek, "sphinx" means "strangler," indicating its relevance for the concept of oral frustration and oral hostility. Oedipus' interaction with the Sphinx reveals characteristics of a mutual oral incorporation. He too desires to destroy her. Perhaps he wishes to participate in her power by replacing her.

Actually, the frustrating early mother–infant relationship—for example, Jocasta's crime in not fulfilling her duty as a mother, her wish to kill her child in order to save her husband, which is an unforgivable crime from the standpoint of matriarchal society—helped set up the sequence of events that eventually led to her husband's, her own, and her son's destruction. Oedipus is ultimately reconciled or fused with the primordial mother by disappearing into a fissure in the earth, finally appeasing the externalized, persecutory maternal objects, the Erinyes, or Harpies, who relentlessly pursue him.

Though the events and characters of the Oedipus trilogy have by now been multiply interpreted, one might say that, among other meanings, the incestuous relationship between Jocasta and Oedipus, a much younger man, may have fulfilled a guilty desire on Jocasta's part to make up for her earlier rejection, which of course only led to Oedipus' eventual emasculation and exile.

Writers of the Romantic era, experts on the theme of "pleasure in pain," project the female as unattainable and ungiving, or reflect ill-concealed hatred and malevolence toward women. Of interest in the lives of many is the pervasive incidence of abandonment by mother, either by death or emotional rejection. For example, Poe's mother died when he was three. Poe wrote that the "death of a beautiful woman is the most poetical topic in the world" (Praz, 1956). Byron's father died when the poet was three, subjecting Byron, according to his biographer, to his mother's alternatingly violent temper and excessive "tenderness." De Sade's mother sent him as a young child of four to live with his grandmother and at six shipped him off to an uncle (Cleugh, 1951). Keats' father died when he was six. His mother remarried, left her second husband and her children, then disappeared for several years. Keats wrote that his greatest misfortune since childhood was that he had no mother (Ward, 1963). Perhaps he was repulsed by his mother's remarriage, as was Hamlet, whose father was "but two months dead." Furthermore, Keats was haunted by the fear that any woman he loved would "play him false" and leave him.[1] There is a constant recurrence in his poetry of a

---

[1] Keats' mother loved and indulged him more than her other children, only to withdraw after his father's death.

connection of food with love, suggesting his mother's abandonment was a revival of an earlier oral trauma. Sexual pleasure in "Endymion" is referred to as "feeding" at the breast. In a letter to Fanny Brawne, Keats' sweetheart and unconsummated love, he speaks of trying to "wean" himself from her. He nursed and fed his mother when she finally returned; then she died. Love, for him, thus, often emerges as a prelude to death.

Third, the female may be avoided or feared because her lack of a penis engenders castration fear or dread in the male. Conversely, the phallic[1] attributes of women may be feared. Mother's breasts or nipples may be perceived as intrusive. She may be viewed as anally penetrative. During the bowel-training period, D. and his mother constantly battled over toilet training, which eventuated in masochistic submission on his part to the administering of enemas by his mother. He "gladly" took these to avoid her wrath. E.'s mother was genitally intrusive, i.e., E. had vaginal discharges as a child that her mother tended. Also, E. sought out a close relative, a physician, who often acted as a mother-surrogate, to administer an abortion.

C.'s mother was present at a physical check-up, where he was told by the physician that he had undescended testicles, a highly traumatic experience for him, since he

---

[1]In her explorations of embryonic female morphology, Sherfey (1966) claims that embryologically speaking, mammalian sexual organs are "anatomically and physiologically female structures" with all the potentialities for development in the female growth pattern. The penis is an exaggerated clitoris, the scrotum is derived from the labia majora; indeed modern embryology "calls for an Adam-out-of-Eve myth." Female structures develop into male sexual organs by the stimulus of fetal androgens by the end of the second fetal month. A discussion of Sherfey's paper by Heiman (1968) refutes her claims to "female primacy" and "masculine deviations," indicating she has, in his opinion, "completely misunderstood and misinterpreted the facts established by embryology."

felt his mother's presence both visually penetrative and emotionally undermining. Also emotionally invasive was B.'s mother, who would listen to her conversations on the telephone, and F.'s mother, who called her daughter's friends to check up on her. Other mothers may appear verbally inundating, controlling, and intrusive.

When the female is dominant and powerful as wife and mother, she may be projected as unfeminine, castrating, dangerous, phallic, Medusa-like. The Medusa, with her snake hair and protruding eyes, tongue, and teeth, probably represents a maternal image of the phallic phase. Distorted preoedipal images thus tend to confound the child in the identification process. Neumann (1963) notes that the destructive side of the feminine, the "destructive and deadly womb," appears most frequently "in the . . . form of a mouth bristling with teeth." This is observed in an African statuette where, instead of the tooth-studded womb, we have substituted a gnashing mask. The latter symbolism is also seen in an Aztec likeness of the death goddess, furnished with a variety of knives and sharp teeth. The "vagina dentata" theme is found in North American Indian mythology, where a meat-eating fish resides in the vagina of the "Terrible Mother," breaks the teeth out of her vagina, and changes her into a woman.

Fourth, the mother may be seen as ensnarer or devourer if her sheltering, nurturing role is not relinquished at the optimal period for separation-individuation in the child's development. The danger of captivity, equated with the parent's reluctance to release the child, is a frequent theme in fairy tales, i.e., in the depiction of mother as giver of life but also as a container who can hold fast, or draw back the life of the individual into herself. Life and birth are inevitably bound up with death and destruction. The Temple of Kali in Calcutta is noted for its hundreds of daily blood sacrifices. To the Goddess Kali is due the life blood of all creatures, "since it is she who has bestowed it" (Neumann, 1963).

How then does one fuse the bad and good mother into a unitary image? The child absorbs the mother relationship in its numerous nuances; he perceives that at times mother may be nurturing, tender, helpful, playful, sensual, cuddling, yet, at other times, preoccupied, involved with others, objective, hurtful, distant, restraining, or depriving. These latter attitudes are necessary on occasion and enable the infant to learn toleration of frustration. When the oral gestalt is a generally benign one, variations in mother's availability are relatively acceptable. Optimal development in ensuing growth periods depends upon the continuing good will of the mother, the nature of the father relationship, the parents' marital patterns, and the relationship with siblings.

Otherwise, as noted in our clinical illustrations—which evidence a unique constellation of maternal ambivalence and/or paternal cruelty, unavailability in the early developmental phases, and depreciated parental images for identification—a masochistic orientation may eventuate. Like patients in their dreams and free associations, poets and artists project unresolved childhood conflicts in their choice of themes and images. Their work may reveal, among many other things, varied perceptions of parents, sometimes overidealized as omnipotently powerful, at other times caricatured as monsters, devourers, or cruel oppressors. These images are particularly ambiguous and exaggerated in regard to the preverbal, preoedipal mother relationship. The emergent attitude seems contingent on the child's, patient's, or artist's total development at a particular nodal point.

The cultural–historical matrix can serve as backdrop

to, or can facilitate, specific, behavioral interactions within a particular group. We have concentrated here on the parent–child relationship and on the family, which in our epoch acts as the central transmitter of culture. It can thus function as a catalyst or prototype for later masochistic orientations, both intrapsychic and interpersonal. But the basic family unit provides us only with a fundamental instance of what our culture catalyzes on a larger scale. Currently an extraordinary amount of suffering and alienation is evident in all social and group patterns. Despite religious, humanistic, or democratic strictures inveighing against man's inhumanity to man, contradictions abound and inundate us. Killing and violence are considered abhorrent, but we are desensitized to their everyday occurrence. We observe and participate in warfare, in the scapegoating of minority groups, in predatory crimes, in the humiliations of poverty, and in various other indices of inequality. Our desensitization is illuminated by a recent psychological experiment: Subjects were told that in the interest of a research project—rather Machiavellian in design—they were to administer shocks of varying intensities to persons they could not see. They proceeded to do so even when they were told that increases of shock might be injurious to the recipients (Milgrim, 1963).

Perhaps the crucial variable operating in this experiment is the distance of experimenter from subject and of the subjects administering, from those receiving, shock.[1]

---

[1] Milgrim's research on obedience shows that most people will follow without question instructions to harm others if the instructions come from those in authority and the situation renders the tormentor dependent on the authority. Should the victim be remote or faceless the tendency to inflict pain on command will override moral considerations to a greater extent. Willingness to commit destructive acts is linked with the temptation to ascribe responsibility for the decision and the results onto the experimenter.

This experiment could be used as a paradigm for other interactions in modern life. The distance between the worker and his product, between the ownership of means of production and worker or consumer, may obviate any need for individual responsibility on all these levels. Similarly, the immense separation in modern warfare between aggressor and victim, evidenced in chemical warfare or in mass bombing of cities; between the powers that be and ordinary citizens, may be at the core of man's insensitivity to and alienation from his fellows. This seems in part the substrate for an Eichmann, who claimed only to be executing orders from above.

References

Abraham, K. (1948), *Selected Papers on Psychoanalysis.* The first pregenital stage of the libido (1916) and A short study of the development of the libido viewed in light of mental disorders (1924). London: Hogarth Press.

Adorno, T. (1950), *The Authoritarian Personality.* New York: Harper and Brothers.

Alexander, F. (1924), *The Psychoanalysis of the Total Personality.* New York: Nervous and Mental Disease Publishing Co.

Ariès, P. (1960), *Centuries of Childhood,* trans. R. Baldick. New York: Vintage Books.

Arlow, J. A. (1961), Ego psychology and the study of mythology. *J. Am. Psychoanal. Assoc.*, 9: 371–393.

Bach, S., and Schwartz, L. (1972), A dream of the Marquis de Sade. Psychoanalytic reflections on the narcissistic trauma, decompensation and the reconstruction of a delusional self. *J. Am. Psychoanal. Assoc.*, 20: 451–476.

Bak, B. C. (1946), Masochism in paranoia. *Psychoanal. Q.*, 15: 285–301.

Balter, L. (1969), The mother as source of power. *Psychoanal. Q.*, 38: 217–274.

Beck, A. T. (1967), *Depression: Clinical, Experimental and Theoretical Aspects.* New York: Harper and Row.

Bergler, E. (1949), *The Basic Neurosis.* New York: Grune & Stratton.

Berliner, B. (1940), Libido and reality in masochism. *Psychoanal. Q.*, 9: 322–333.

———— (1942), The concept of masochism. *Psychoanal. Rev.*, 29: 386–400.

———— (1947), On some psychodynamics of masochism. *Psychoanal. Q.*, 16: 459–471.

———— (1958), The role of object relations in moral masochism. *Psychoanal. Q.*, 27: 38–56.

Bernstein, I. (1957), The role of narcissism in moral masochism. *Psychoanal. Q.*, 26: 358–377.

Bieber, I. (1966), Sadism and masochism. In *American Handbook of Psychiatry*, ed. S. Arieti, 3: 256–270. New York: Basic Books.

Bloch, D. (1965), Feelings that kill: The effect of the wish for infanticide in neurotic depression. *Psychoanal. Rev.*, 52: 51–66.

Blumstein, A. (1959), Masochism and fantasies of preparing to be incorporated. *J. Am. Psychoanal. Assoc.*, 7: 292–298.

Bonaparte, M. (1953), *Female Sexuality*. New York: International Universities Press.

Bowlby, J. (1966), *Deprivation and Maternal Care*. New York: Schocken Books.

Brenman, M. (1952), On teasing and being teased and the problems of "moral masochism." In *The Psychoanalytic Study of the Child*, 7:264–285. New York: International Universities Press.

Brenner, C. (1959), The masochistic character. *J. Am. Psychoanal. Assoc.*, 7:197–226.

——— (1972), The psychoanalytic concept of aggression. *Int. J. Psychoanal.*, 52:137–144.

Brody, S. (1956), *Patterns of Mothering*. New York: International Universities Press.

Bromberg, W. (1955), Mothers of moral masochists. *Am. J. Orthopsychiatry*, 25:802–809.

Brunswick, R. M. (1940), The pre-oedipal phase of libido development. *Psychoanal. Q.*, 9:293–319.

Bychowski, G. (1959), Some aspects of masochistic involvement. *J. Am. Psychoanal. Assoc.*, 7:248–273.

Cleugh, J. (1951), *The Marquis and the Chevalier*. London: Andrew Melrose.

De Beauvoir, S. (1953a), *The Second Sex*. New York: Alfred Knopf.

——— (1953b), *Marquis de Sade*. New York: Grove Press.

De Monchy, R. (1950), Masochism as a pathological and as a normal phenomenon in the human mind. *Int. J. Psychoanal.*, 31:95–97.

De Sade, Marquis (1785), *The 120 Days of Sodom*, trans. A. Wainhouse and R. Seaver. New York: Grove Press, 1966.

——— (1791), *Justine*. In *Three Complete Novels*, trans. R. Seaver and A. Wainhouse. New York: Grove Press, 1965.

Deutsch, H. (1944), *The Psychology of Women*. New York: Grune & Stratton.

Dollard, J., *et al.* (1939), *Frustration and Aggression*. New Haven: Yale University Press.

Dooley, L. (1941), The relation of humor to masochism. *Psychoanal. Rev.*, 28:37–46.

Eidelberg, L. (1959), Humiliation in masochism. *J. Am. Psychoanal. Assoc.*, 7:274–283.

Eisenbud, R. J. (1967), Masochism revisited. *Psychoanal. Rev.*, 54:5–27.

Erikson, E. (1950), *Childhood and Society*. New York: Norton.

Escalona, S. (1968), *The Roots of Individuality*. Chicago: Aldine.

Fenichel, O. (1935), A critique of the death instinct. In *Collected Papers*, I:363–373. New York: Norton, 1953.

———— (1945), *The Psychoanalytic Theory of Neuroses*. New York: Norton.

Ferenczi, S. (1909), Introjection and transference. In *Sex in Psychoanalysis*, 35–94. New York: Basic Books.

Flugel, J. C. (1961), *Man, Morals and Society*. New York: Viking Press.

Forrest, T. (1966), *Paternal roots of female character development. Contemp. Psychoanal.*, 3:21–39.

Framo, J. (1965), Rationale and techniques of intensive family therapy. In *Intensive Family Therapy,* ed. I. Boszormenyi-Nagy and J. L. Framo, 143–213. New York: Harper and Row.

Freud, A. (1949), Aggression in relation to emotional development: Normal and pathological. In *The Psychoanalytic Study of the Child*, 3–4:37–43. New York: International Universities Press.

Freud, S. (1900), The interpretation of dreams. In *Basic*

Writings of Sigmund Freud. New York: Modern Library, 1938.

———— (1905), *Three Essays on the Theory of Sexuality.* New York: Nervous and Mental Disease Monographs.

———— (1908), On the sexual theories of children. In *Collected Papers*, 2:59–76. London: Hogarth Press.

———— (1910), Contributions to the psychology of love. A special type of object choice made by men. In *Collected Papers*, 4:192–202. London: Hogarth Press.

———— (1911), Formulations regarding the two principles in mental functioning. In *Collected Papers*, 4:13–22. London: Hogarth Press.

———— (1912), Contributions to the psychology of love. The most prevalent form of degradation in erotic life. In *Collected Papers*, 2:203–217. London: Hogarth Press.

———— (1914), On narcissism. An introduction. In *Collected Papers*, 4:30–60. London: Hogarth Press.

———— (1915a), Some character types met with in psychoanalytic work. In *Collected Papers*, 4:318–344. London: Hogarth Press.

———— (1915b), Instincts and their vicissitudes. In *Collected Papers*, 4:60–84. London: Hogarth Press.

———— (1919), A child is being beaten. A Contribution to the study of the origin of sexual perversions. In *Collected Papers,* 2:172–201. London: Hogarth Press.

———— (1920), *Beyond the Pleasure Principle.* London: Hogarth Press.

———— (1922), *Group Psychology and the Analysis of the Ego.* New York: Liveright.

———— (1923), *The Ego and the Id.* London: Hogarth Press, 1927.

———— (1924), The economic problem in masochism. In *Collected Papers*, 2:255–268. London: Hogarth Press.

——— (1930), *Civilization and Its Discontents*. London: Hogarth Press.

——— (1933), The psychology of women. In *New Introductory Lectures on Psychoanalysis*, 153–185. New York: Norton.

——— (1937), Analysis terminable and interminable. In *Collected Papers*, 5:316–357. London: Hogarth Press.

——— (1940), *Outline of Psychoanalysis*. London: Hogarth Press.

Fromm, E. (1941), *Escape from Freedom*. New York: Farrar and Rinehart.

——— (1964), *The Heart of Man*. New York: Harper and Row.

——— (1972), The Erich Fromm theory of aggression. *New York Times Magazine*, February 27, 1972.

Fromm-Reichmann, F. (1959), *Psychoanalysis and Psychotherapy*, 221–277. Chicago: University of Chicago Press.

Gero, G. (1962), Sadism, masochism and aggression. Their role in symptom formation. *Psychoanal. Q.*, 31:31–42.

Gornick, V. (1971), Why women fear success. *New York Times Magazine*, December 20, 1971.

Graves, R. (1959), *The Greek Myths*. Baltimore: Penguin.

Greenacre, P. (1952), *Trauma, Growth and Personality*. New York: Norton.

Greenson, R. (1967), *The Technique and Practice of Psychoanalysis*. New York: International Universities Press.

Grinker, R. R. (1957), On identification. *Int. J. Psychoanal.*, 38:379–489.

Hartmann, H. (1964), *Essays on Ego Psychology*. New York: International Universities Press.

———, Kris, E., and Lowenstein, R. (1949), Notes on the theory of aggression. In *The Psychoanalytic Study of the Child*, 3–4:9–36. New York: International Universities Press.

————, and Lowenstein, R. (1962), Notes on the superego. In *The Psychoanalytic Study of the Child*, 17:42–81. New York: International Universities Press.

Heiman, M. (1968), Discussion of M. J. Sherfey: "The evolution of female sexuality in relation to psychoanalytic theory." *J. Am. Psychoanal. Assoc.*, 16:405–449.

Hess, E. (1962), *Ethology: An Approach toward the Complete Analysis of Behavior*. In *New Directions in Psychology*, 157–267. New York: Holt, Rinehart and Winston.

Hoch, P. (1959), Masochism: Clinical considerations. In *Individual and Family Dynamics*, ed. Jules Masserman, 42–43. New York: Grune & Stratton.

Horney, K. (1939), *New Ways in Psychoanalysis*. New York: Norton.

Jacobson, E. (1953), The affects and their pleasure–unpleasure qualities in relation to the psychic discharge processes. In *Drives, Affects, Behavior*, ed. R. L. Lowenstein, 38–66. New York: International Universities Press.

———— (1971), *Depression*. New York: International Universities Press.

Kacera, C. (1959), On teething. *J. Am. Psychoanal. Assoc.*, 7:284–291.

Kardiner, A. (1945), *Psychological Frontiers of Society*. New York: Columbia University Press.

Kelman, H. (1959), Masochism and self-realization. In *Individual and Family Dynamics*, ed. Jules Masserman, 21–30. New York: Grune & Stratton.

Kernberg, O. (1965), Notes on countertransference. *J. Am. Psychoanal. Assoc.*, 13:38–57.

———— (1972), Treatment of borderline patients. In *Tactics and Techniques in Psychoanalytic Therapy*, 254–290. New York: Science House.

Klein, M. (1940), *Contributions to Psychoanalysis*. London: Hogarth Press.

Kohut, H. (1966), Forms and transformations of narcissism. *J. Am. Psychoanal. Assoc.*, 14: 243–272.

———— (1971), *The Analysis of the Self.* New York: International Universities Press.

Krafft-Ebing, R. (1900), *Psychopathia Sexualis.* New York: Rebman.

Lewis, H. B. (1971), *Shame and Guilt in Neuroses.* New York: International Universities Press.

Lichtenstein, H. (1961), Identity and sexuality. *J. Am. Psychoanal. Assoc.*, 9: 179–260.

Lidz, T. (1957), The intra-familial environment of the schizophrenic. I. The father. *Psychiatry*, 20: 329–342.

Lowenstein, R. (1957), A contribution to the psychoanalytic theory of masochism. *J. Am. Psychoanal. Assoc.*, 5: 197–234.

Mahler, M. (1952), On child psychosis and schizophrenia: Autistic and symbiotic infantile psychosis. In *The Psychoanalytic Study of the Child*, 7: 286–306.

Malcove, L. (1945), Margaret E. Fries' research in problems of infancy and childhood. In *The Psychoanalytic Study of the Child*, 1: 405–414. New York: International Universities Press.

May, R. (1972), *Power and Innocence.* New York: Norton.

Menaker, E. (1942), The masochistic factor in the psychoanalytic situation. *Psychoanal. Q.*, 11: 171–186.

———— (1953), Masochism, a defense reaction. *Psychoanal. Q.*, 22: 205–220.

Menninger, K. (1938), *Man against Himself.* New York: Harcourt Brace.

Milgrim, S. (1963), Behavioral study of obedience. *J. Abnorm. Soc. Psychol.*, 67: 371–378.

Miller, N. E., et al. (1941), The frustration–aggression hypothesis. *Psychol. Rev.*, 18: 102–115.

Millet, J. (1959), Masochism: Psychogenesis and therapeutic principles. In *Individual and Family Dynamics*, ed. Jules Masserman, 44–52. New York: Grune & Stratton.

Mitchell, C. (1968), The therapeutic field in the treatment of families in conflict. Recurrent themes in literature and clinical practice. In *New Directions in Mental Health*, Bernard Reiss, 69–99. New York: Grune & Stratton.

Murphy, G., and Murphy, L. (1937), *Experimental Social Psychology*. New York: Harper and Bros.

Nacht, S., and Racamier, P. C. (1960), Symposium on depressive illness. II. Depressive states. *Int. J. Psychoanal.*, 41:481–496.

Neumann, E. (1963), *The Great Mother*. New York: Pantheon.

Nunberg, H. (1955), *Principles of Psychoanalysis*. New York: International Universities Press.

Nydes, J. (1963), The paranoid-masochistic character. *Psychoanal. Rev.*, 50:55–91.

Piers, G., and Singer, H. (1953), *Shame and Guilt*. Springfield: Charles C Thomas.

Praz, M. (1956), *The Romantic Agony*. New York: Meridian Books.

Rado, S. (1959), Panel discussion on masochism. In *Individual and Family Dynamics*, ed. Jules Masserman, 53–56. New York: Grune & Stratton.

Reich, A. (1940), A contribution to the psychoanalysis of extreme submissiveness in women. *Psychoanal. Q.*, 9:470–480.

Reich, W. (1933), *Character Analysis*. New York: Orgone Institute Press.

Reik, T. (1941), *Masochism in Modern Man*. New York: Farrar and Strauss.

Ribble, M. (1943), *The Rights of Infants, Early Psycho-*

logical Needs and Their Satisfaction. New York: Columbia University Press.

Ricoeur, P. (1970), *Freud and Philosophy.* New Haven: Yale University Press.

Rubinfine, D. (1965), On beating fantasies. *Int. J. Psychoanal.,* 46:315–322.

Sacher-Masoch, L. von (1870), *Venus in Furs,* trans. F. Savage. New York: Belmont Books, 1965.

Salzman, L. (1959), Masochism: A review of theory and therapy. In *Individual and Family Dynamics,* ed. Jules Masserman, 1–20. New York: Grune & Stratton.

———— (1960), Masochism and psychopathy as adaptive behavior. *J. Ind. Psychol.,* 16:182–188.

———— (1962), *Developments in Psychoanalysis.* New York: Grune & Stratton.

Schactel, E. (1959), *Metamorphosis.* New York: Basic Books.

Schafer, R. (1954), *Psychoanalytic Interpretations in Rorschach Testing.* New York: Grune & Stratton.

Schuster, D. B. (1966), Notes on "A child is being beaten." *Psychoanal. Q.,* 35:357–367.

Sherfey, M. J. (1966), The evolution of female sexuality in relation to psychoanalytic theory. *J. Am. Psychoanal. Assoc.,* 14:28–128.

Solnit, A. J. (1972), Aggression: A view of theory building in psychoanalysis. *J. Am. Psychoanal. Assoc.,* 20:435–451.

Spitz, R. (1945), Hospitalism. In *The Psychoanalytic Study of the Child,* 1:53–74. New York: International Universities Press.

———— (1951), Psychogenic diseases in infancy. In *The Psychoanalytic Study of the Child,* 6:255–275. New York: International Universities Press.

Stone, L. (1971), Reflections on the psychoanalytic concept of aggression. *Psychoanal. Q.*, 40:195–244.

Storr, A. (1971), *Human Aggression*. New York: Atheneum.

Sullivan, H. S. (1946), Conceptions of modern psychiatry. Reprinted from *Psychiatry*, 3:1–147, 1940.

Szasz, T. (1957), *Pain and Pleasure*. New York: Basic Books.

Thompson, C. (1959), The interpersonal approach to the clinical problems of masochism. In *Individual and Family Dynamics*, ed. Jules Masserman, 31–37. New York: Grune & Stratton.

Waelder, R. (1936), The principle of multiple function. *Psychoanal. Q.*, 15:45–62.

——— (1964), *Basic Theory of Psychoanalysis*. New York: Schocken Books.

Ward, A. (1963), *John Keats*. New York: Viking Press.

Wilson, E. (1965), The vogue of the Marquis de Sade. In *The Bit between My Teeth*, 158–173. New York: Farrar and Strauss.

Winnicott, D. W. (1958), *Collected Papers*. London: Tavistock Publications.

——— (1965), *Maturation Processes and the Facilitating Environment*. New York: International Universities Press.

Wittels, F. (1937), The mystery of masochism. *Psychoanal. Rev.*, 24:139–149.

Wynne, L. (1965), Some indications and contra-indications for exploratory family therapy. In *Intensive Family Therapy*, ed. I. Boszormenyi-Nagy and J. L. Framo, 289–322. New York: Harper and Row.

INDEX

abilities, 88
Abraham, K., 110
accidents, 85
acting out, 147, 148, 154, 157
activities, inhibition of, 163
Adam and Eve, 211, 217
adaptive-instrumental situations, 87
admiration, 152
Adorno, T., 200 n.
aggression, 32–34, 47, 53, 60, 89, 107–
  126, 129, 147
  oral, 151
  pregenital, 151
aggressor
  identification with, 124, 147
  seduction of, 56–57
Alexander, F., 31

alienation, 181, 220
  cultural, 205
ambition, 55
ambivalence, 19–20, 81, 85, 86, 104
America, 141, 201 n., 203
anal phase, 110
anal-sadistic organization, 22, 37
analyst
  See psychoanalyst
anger, 124, 157, 171, 175
Anna Karenina, 202
annihilation, 119, 121
anxiety, 39, 48, 154
Ariés, P., 207
Arlow, J. A., 213 n.
asceticism, 52
atactic behavior, 39

Athena, 211
atonement, 131
attitudes, projective, 125
attraction, 171
autarchic omnipotence, 52
authoritarianism, 48, 123
autoaggression, 133
autoerotism, 133

Bach, S., 121, 122
Bak, B. C., 101
Balter, L., 215
beating, 20 ff., 28 f., 39, 42, 101
    and sex, 37–38
Beck, A. T., 98
behavior, 184, 220
Bergler, E., 51, 52
Berliner, B., 49, 50, 60, 88, 96–97,
    99–100, 125, 146–147
Bernstein, I., 54
"Beyond the Pleasure Principle," 23,
    24
Bieber, I., 36, 37, 50, 83, 116, 140, 148
bisexuality, 112
blackmailing, 97, 125
Bleuler, E., 19
Bloch, D., 206 n.
Blumstein, A., 53–54
Bonaparte, M., 37
bondage, sexual, 13
Bowlby, J., 82
Brenman, M., 47, 58–61, 97, 125
Brenner, C., 45, 113, 160–162
Brody, S., 82
Bromberg, W., 86
Brunswick, R. M., 112
Bychowsky, G., 53
Byron, Lord, 216

cannibalism, 18
capabilities, underestimation of, 163
case studies, 63–79, 160–195
castration, 26, 35, 36, 101, 112, 113
celibacy, 208
character, masochistic, 38–41, 64
child, 26, 198, 199
    battered, 207
    killing of, 206
    psychotic, 102

childbirth, 35, 202
"A Child Is Being Beaten," 20, 28
Christianity, 12
Civilization and Its Discontents, 114, 115,
    129
class, 118
Cleugh, J., 216
coercion, 125
coitus, 35
communication, 135
complicity, 133
compromise, 58
conscience, 25, 115
    sadistic, 28
contempt, 152
control, 60
countertransference, 155–156, 177,
    195
criminality, 55–56
cruelty
    component, 18–19
    paternal, 219
culture, 197 ff.

David Copperfield, 206
death
    instinct, 23, 24, 26, 31–34, 119, 137,
        144
    wish, 112
de Beauvoir, S., 131, 207, 213
decompensation, narcissistic, 121
defeat, 60, 185
defense, 49–50, 60
    masochistic, 83, 156, 158
Delilah, 210–211
delusion, 101
Demeter, 209
de Monchy, R., 44
denial, 155
dependence, 44, 88, 116, 171
depression, 44, 96–98, 147–149
depressive phase, 151
deprivation, 59, 60
    emotional, 176
de Sade, Marquis, 13, 121–123, 212
desertion, 175
destiny, 41
destruction, 32, 46, 115, 118, 121, 129

Deutsch, H., 35, 167, 177
developmental patterns, 81–93
Dickens, Charles, 206
differences, sexual, 90
differential diagnosis, 95–105
difficulties, interpersonal, 191
disappointment, 203
  oral, 30
discharge, affective, 131
discipline, 20
disturbances, personality, 152
Dollard, J., 114
Dooley, L., 46
dreams, 168
drives, 46, 51, 132, 137

"The Economic Problem in Masochism," 25, 129
education, 184
ego, 24, 27, 47, 50, 54, 55, 130
  deformation of, 163
  functions, 97
  ideal, 25, 43, 44
  instincts, 33, 114
  lack of, 103
  psychology, 33–34, 59
  reduced, 46
  suffering of, 99
The Ego and the Id, 24, 115
Eichmann, A., 221
Eidelberg, L., 52–53, 149
Eisenbud, R. J., 60, 148–149
embeddedness, 137
"Endymion," 217
England, 207
environment, 53
Erikson, E., 110
Eros, 33, 115
erotism, anal, 110–111
Escalona, S., 82
Europe, 118, 141
excitation, 138
exhibitionism, 40
exploitation, 60, 117
"Extreme Submissiveness in Women," 34

failure, 19, 89

family, 139, 199, 203, 206 ff.
  as transmitter of culture, 220
fantasy, 20 ff., 28–29, 37–38, 46, 123
  phallic, 111–112
fascism, 116, 118
fate, 28
father, 21, 64–65, 70–71, 74, 76, 86–88, 89, 91, 101, 111, 120, 165, 179, 182, 186, 189
  despotic, 200–201
  identification with, 112
  passive-aggressive, 203
  weak, 204
  See also parents
Fechner, G., 127
feelings, autonomous, 139
females,
  See women
Fenichel, O., 33, 35, 41–42, 96, 99, 131
Ferenczi, S., 198
feudalism, 48, 208
Flugel, J. C., 212 n.
food, and love, 217
formations, masochistic, 92–93
"Formulations Regarding the Two Principles in Mental Functioning," 127
Forrest, T., 90
Framo, J., 91
freedom, 48
Freud, A., 111 n.
Freud, S., 11, 13–15, 17–30 *passim*, 37, 38, 43, 55, 60, 68 n., 72 n., 96, 98–99, 107–126 *passim*, 127 ff., 137 ff., 143–144, 154, 199, 214
Fromm, E., 48, 116–120
Fromm-Reichmann, F., 102
frustration, 29, 131, 193
  oral, 89
functions
  bodily, 134

gain, 136
Gero, G., 50–51, 111, 112
giving, 59
goals, 190–191
God, 41, 200 n.

goddesses, ancient, 211
Gornick, V., 89
gratification, 13, 41, 138, 151
Graves, R., 211
Greco-Romans, 209, 210 n.
Greenacre, P., 128 n.
Greenson, R., 194
grievances, 191
Grinker, R. R., 82
guilt, 25, 27, 43–44, 45, 46, 55, 60, 115, 146, 153

Hamlet, 216
happiness, 129
Hartmann, H., 33–34, 113, 129
Heiman, M., 217 n.
helplessness, 45
Hess, E., 82
heterosexuality, 90, 176
Himmler, H., 117
Hitler, A., 119, 120, 121
Hoch, P., 95
homeostasis, 132
homosexuality, 177
Horney, K., 34
hostility, 147
humiliation, 35, 40–41, 52–53
humor, 46–49
hypnosis, 144
hypocrisy, 42

idealization, 152
idealized parent-image, 152
identification, 91, 112
identity, 203
    assertion of, 181
illness, 85
impotence, social, 205
imprinting, 82
impulse, 96
inadequacy, 117
incest, 36, 88
incestuous symbiosis, 119, 120
incorporation, 53–54
independence, 45
Indians, 218
Industrial Revolution, 206–207
injury, bodily, 136
    lesser, 39

instincts, 23
    aggressive, 50–51
    defused, 33
    dual, 32
    sexual, 50–51
"Instincts and Their Vicissitudes," 19, 98
integrative approach, 58–60
integrative-expressive areas, 87
intellect, 88
intercourse, 68
internalization, 112
interpersonal approach, 57–58
The Interpretation of Dreams, 127
introjects, 193
Isis, 210
isolation, 117

Jacobson, E., 131–132, 135 n., 149–150
jealousy, 22
Jocasta, 206, 215, 216
Judaism, 73–74
Judith, 211
justice, 55
Justine, 121

Kacera, C., 110
Kali, 211, 218–219
Kardiner, A., 48–49
Keats, J., 212, 216–217
Kelman, H., 139, 147
Kernberg, O., 151
Klein, M., 32, 52
Kohut, H., 55, 56, 121, 152, 153
Kraepelin, E., 95
Krafft-Ebing, R., 11, 12, 13, 17, 37, 60, 109

"La Belle Dame Sans Merci," 212
Laius, 206
Lawrence, D. H., 204
Leviticus, 207
Lewis, H. B., 38, 43–44
libido, 32, 109, 113, 114
    narcissistic, 53
Lichtenstein, H., 82
Lidz, T., 86 n., 87

life, 137, 139
Lorenz, K., 115
loss, 60, 97
love, 36, 39, 47, 49, 50, 52, 58, 100, 171
Lowenstein, R., 36, 42, 56–57, 66 n., 113, 132–134

Malcove, L., 85 n.
males
    See men
manic-depressive reaction, 110
martyrdom, 52
masculinity complex, 23
masochism, active and passive, 13
    and aggression, 107–126
    and criminality, 55–56
    cultural implications, 197–221
    as defense, 49–50
    and depression, 96–98
    developmental patterns, 81–93
    diagnosis, 95–105
    erotogenic, 26
    feminine, 34–36
    formations, 92–93
    Freud on, 17–30
    history, 11 ff.
    and humor, 46–49
    and incorporation, 53–54
    literature on, 31 ff.
    moral, 27–29, 41
    and narcissism, 54–55
    as normal, 44–46
    and obsessive-compulsive neurosis, 98–100
    and paranoid mechanisms, 87, 100–104
    physiological basis, 128
    as perversion, 36–37
    psychic, 51–52
    and psychotherapy, 143–195
    and sadism, 107–126
    symptom formation, 50–51
masochistic reaction, in psychotherapy, 145
mastery, 60
    loss of, 136
masturbation, 21, 26, 169

May, R., 118 n.
mechanisms, oral, 51
Medusa, 211, 213, 218
megalomania, 101, 119
melancholia, 115
men, 90, 91
Menaker, E., 50, 60, 84, 104, 144–146
Menninger, K., 31
Middle Ages, 48, 207, 208, 210
Milgrim, S., 220
Miller, N. E., 114
Millet, J., 52
misery, 41
Mitchell, C., 206
morality, 27
mortification, 45, 52–53
mother, 23, 29, 35, 42, 52, 65–66, 69–70, 73, 76, 82, 84 ff., 86, 91, 102, 111, 164, 166, 167, 168, 171, 177, 179–180, 182, 185–186, 214
    ambivalent, 199, 219
    as ensnarer or devourer, 218
    good and bad, 103, 104–105, 209 ff., 219
    matriarchal, 203
    and nourishment, 214–215
    phallic, 112
    superhuman, 120
    See also parents
mother-child relationship, 14, 28, 30
motivational hierarchy, 61
murder, 33, 123
Murphy, G., 19 n.
Murphy, L., 19 n.
mutiliation, 26

Nacht, S., 98, 103, 128 n.
narcissism, 54–55, 151–152
    malignant, 119, 120
narcissistic mortification, 52–53
necrophilia, 119, 120
needs, 134
negative therapeutic reaction, 143, 194
Neumann, E., 209, 210, 218, 219
neurosis, 31, 44
neutralization, 33
normalcy, 44–46

Nunberg, H., 32
nursing, 84
Nydes, J., 87, 100–101, 125

obedience, 220
object, 98, 102
  loss of, 54
  relationships, 135
obsessive-compulsive neurosis, 98–100,
  111
Oedipus, 206, 215, 216
Oedipus complex, 14, 19, 24–25, 45,
  54, 96, 112, 204
  desexualizing, 28
  infantile, 30, 149
  omnipotence, 53
"On the Sexual Theories of Children,"
  19
The 120 Days of Sodom, 121, 123
oral phase, 110
Outline of Psychoanalysis, 130
overstimulation, 131

pain, 13, 15, 20, 37, 49, 116, 117, 129
  and pleasure, 127–141, 216
pain-dependency, 132
Pandora, 211
paranoia, 44, 100–104, 147
parent-child relationship, 54–55
parents, 67–68, 197 ff., 204
  depriving, 139
  reunion with, 133
pathology, narcissistic, 121
patterns, nonverbal and verbal, 158
penetration, fear of, 171
personality, masochistic, 63–64
  parental, 199 ff.
perversion, 18, 35–37, 49, 96, 123
phallic period, 37
Piers, G., 43
play, 133
pleasure, 15, 21, 40, 56–57
  in pain, 127–141, 216
  primary model, 134
  sexual, 138
Poe, E. A., 216
position, depressive and paranoid, 32
power, 123, 151

powerlessness, 45
praise, 39
Praz, M., 216
pregenital organization, 22
premasochism, 57
preoedipal relationship, 28, 29, 30,
  60, 199
processes, physiological, 134
prohibition, 131
protomasochism, 57
pseudoaggression, 51
pseudo-debility, 88
pseudo mutuality, 203
psychoanalysis, 11, 33, 144
psychoanalyst, 56
  attitude of, 162 ff.
  character, 151
  dominance of, 144
  global attitude of, 195
  as love object, 174
  sexual overtures toward, 181
  sympathetic involvement of, 148
psychopathology, 55, 83, 95–96
psychosis, 52, 104
psychosomatics, 147
psychotherapy, 143–195
  goals, 190–191
punishment, 20, 36, 37, 40–41, 52, 89,
  99, 130, 132
Puritanism, 48
Pythagoras, 207

Racamier, P. C., 98, 103, 128 n.
Rado, S., 132
rage, 132, 175
reality confrontations, 174
recrimination, 193
regression, 151
Reich, A., 34
Reich, W., 38–39, 90, 96, 130–131
Reik, T., 40–41, 131
rejecting figure, 124
rejection, 56, 146, 171, 174
relationships, heterosexual, 90
religion, 45
Renaissance, 208
repetition compulsion, 23
repression, 51, 53

resources, libidinal, 149
responsibility, 46
retaliation, 32
reversal, 19
Ribble, M., 82
rivalry, 112
"Role of Narcissism in Moral
  Masochism," 54
roles, 173
Rorschach interpretations, 123
Rubinfine, D., 37

sacrifice, 131
sadism, 12–13, 14, 22, 24, 26, 32, 41,
  60, 101, 107–126
  essence of, 117
  oral, 110
  turned on self, 18, 108–109
sadomasochism, 107 ff.
Salzman, L., 45, 55, 97, 154–159,
  162–163
satisfaction, 103
Schactel, E., 136–138
Schafer, R., 123
schizophrenia, 101, 102, 103, 104, 110
Schuster, D. B., 37
Schwartz, L., 121, 122
seduction, 56–57
self, 102
  fragmentation of, 123
  sense of, 125
  turning upon, 126
self-affirmation, 122
  -deprecation, 99–100
  -destruction, 54
  -devaluation, 163
  -esteem, 55
  -image, 91, 139
  -preservation, 129
separation, 60, 101, 136, 171, 174
sessions, frequency of, 150
sexual excitement, 21, 36–37, 128–129
sexuality, male, 109
shame, 43–44, 153
Sherfey, M. J., 217 n.
siblings, 22, 29, 76
sin, 28, 131
Singer, H., 43

skin eroticism, 39, 41, 49
Snow White, 210
Solnit, A. J., 108 n.
Solon, 207
Sons and Lovers, 204
Sophia, 209
Sphinx, 215
Spitz, R., 82, 85
Stone, L., 34
Storr, A., 116
structure defensive, 49–50
struggle, for identity, 172, 173
subject, 98
subjugation, 123
sublimation, 134
submission, 34 ff., 100, 123
  total, 41
success, 19
suffering, 27, 57–58, 86, 125, 140, 146,
  220
suicide, 33, 52, 97, 99, 147
Sullivan, H. S., 57
superego, 24–25, 27, 38, 42, 43, 44, 46,
  49, 54, 99, 112, 153
survival, 197–198
symbiosis, 101, 189
sympathy, 19
symptom formation, 50–51
Szasz, T., 134–136

taboos, 46, 48
tension, 128, 129, 130, 132, 136 n.,
  137, 138, 147, 154
testing, 157
Thanatos, 31, 114, 129
  See also death instinct
Thematic Apperception Test (TAT),
  89 n.
therapy
  See psychotherapy
Thompson, C., 57–58, 147–148
threat, 116, 133, 155
  internalized, 43
Three Contributions to the Theory of Sex,
  17
Tolstoy, L., 202
torture, 52, 99, 117
totalitarianism, 116, 118

transference, 49, 56, 84, 144, 145, 148–149, 151, 152, 177, 181
  masochistic, 159
  mirror, 153
trauma, 153
  oral, 214
traumatic disillusionment, 122
triumph, 38
tug-of-war, 154, 159

unconscious, 25
unpleasure
  See pain
urination, 68

Venus in Furs, 12
victim, 146
violence, 118, 220
Virgin Mary, 210, 211
von Sacher-Masoch, L., 12

Waelder, R., 32, 58
war, 116, 220
Ward, A., 216
West, 12, 48, 207
whipping
  See beating
wife, 214
  submissive, 201–202
Wilson, E., 121
Winnicott, D. W., 82, 214 n.
Wittels, F., 46
women, 34–36, 90, 181
  avoided and feared, 217
  maternal and sexual, 214
  phallic attributes, 217
  rights of, 207 ff.
  roles, attitudes, and characters of, 209 ff.
  Romantic, 212, 216
working through, 147, 160, 183, 191
World War II, 121
Wynne, 203

About the Author

Shirley Panken, Ph.D., is on the editorial staff and is the book review editor of *The Psychoanalytic Review*. She is a member of the National Psychological Association for Psychoanalysis, the Council for Psychoanalytic Psychotherapy, and the American Psychological Association. Dr. Panken is the author of *Virginia Woolf and the "Lust of Creation": A Psychoanalytic Exploration* and numerous articles concerning masochism, countertransference, and the interplay of psychoanalysis and literature. She is a psychoanalyst in private practice in New York City.